THE ULTIMATE
TREASURE HUNT

THE ULTIMATE TREASURE HUNT

A Guide to Supernatural Evangelism
Through Supernatural Encounters

KEVIN DEDMON

DESTINY IMAGE® PUBLISHERS, INC.
P.O. Box 310, Shippensburg, PA 17257-0310

"Speaking to the Purposes of God for this Generation and for the Generations to Come."

This book and all other Destiny Image, Revival Press, Mercy Place, Fresh Bread, Destiny Image Fiction, and Treasure House books are available at Christian bookstores and distributors worldwide.

For a U.S. bookstore nearest you, call 1-800-722-6774.
For more information on foreign distributors, call 717-532-3040.
Or reach us on the Internet: www.destinyimage.com.

ISBN 10: 0-7684-2602-2
ISBN 13: 978-0-7684-2602-1

For Worldwide Distribution, Printed in the U.S.A.

1 2 3 4 5 6 7 8 9 10 11 / 09 08 07

Acknowledgments

Thanks to my amazing wife, Theresa, who believed in me long before I believed in myself. She is the epitome of the Ultimate Treasure Hunter. I love you forever.

Thanks to my two wonderful children, Chad and Alexa, and daughter-in-law (love), Julia, who has been a true "Jewel" in our family.

Chad, you have grown into the man that I envisioned as I gave you your first bath in the delivery room. You are an incredible modern-day revivalist. I am so proud of you.

Alexa, you have watched me get a lot of "No's" on a lot of Treasure Hunts, and you have shared in a lot of divine encounters through your amazing prophetic clues. I have so enjoyed our Treasure Hunts together. I am so proud of you as I see you coming into the confidence of who God made you to be and expressing yourself in your unique factor.

Thanks to Bill Johnson and Kris Vallotton, who have blazed a trail for a naturally supernatural lifestyle. Thank you for allowing me to join in the adventure and explore the avenues that God has put in my heart to expand the Kingdom.

Thanks to Beni Johnson, Marla Baum, and all of the intercessors at Bethel who have paved the way for a revival, Kingdom culture through their prophetic declarations and insights for breakthrough. I never leave home without them.

Thanks to Pam Spinosi, my grammar doctor. You have taught me to say more with less.

Thanks to all of the Treasure Hunters at the various churches where we have done Firestorm conferences, and to Banning Liebscher, who incorporated the Treasure Hunt into the Jesus Culture conferences, allowing me to explore how to effectively activate hundreds of Treasure Hunters at one time.

Finally, thanks to all of the many Treasure Hunters at Bethel Church and in the Bethel School of Supernatural Ministry who have taken so much risk while Treasure Hunting with me over the past four years.

Endorsements

I have worked with Kevin Dedmon for several years. His life story is so unbelievable and his testimonies are so crazy that if I didn't know him myself, I am not sure I would believe this book. But it is all true! Kevin is a modern-day revivalist...a miracle worker with the unique ability to train, equip, and deploy the Body of Christ to do miracles in the marketplace. His life is a catalyst of the supernatural power of God. He is a walking encounter with Heaven, a vortex of healing virtue. His history reads like a chapter out of the Book of Acts.

The testimonies in *The Ultimate Treasure Hunt* will inspire you to live a life of signs and wonders and equip you to bring the Kingdom wherever you go. You will laugh and cry yourself into a new anointing as Kevin shares the stories of his exploits. This book will keep you on the edge of your seat.

It is a must-read for any serious believer, a textbook for those who want to learn how to minister in the gifts of the Spirit. *The Ultimate Treasure Hunt* is destined to become a modern classic, read for generations. I highly recommend this book and its author!

Kris Vallotton
Senior Associate Pastor, Bethel Church
Redding, California

God is raising up a new generation of revivalist for Kingdom expansion in these exciting days. Kevin Dedmon is one of the remarkable leaders of this revival and his book, *The Ultimate Treasure Hunt*, I believe will be a key catalyst to take this global revival to another level. I highly recommend it!

Che Ahn
President of Harvest International Ministry

Revolutionary! Compelling! Cutting edge! This is a book that I couldn't put down! I was intrigued by the creativity and high adventures Kevin Dedmon displayed in *The Ultimate Treasure Hunt*! Everybody loves a game, especially when it is orchestrated and endorsed by the Holy Spirit. His book is full of clues, treasure maps, and divine appointments for a supernatural treasure hunt in the marketplace and ordinary life as believers seek out the Ultimate Treasure: living souls.

This book is a radical training manual for prophetic evangelism, coupled with amazing stories and biblical truths that shatter old religious mind-sets about evangelism. His fresh approach and unreligious language has unique revelation!

It is also a clarion call to mobilize the troops in every arena of life to bring salvation, healing, and deliverance.

Kevin is equipping modern-day "Bravehearts" and releasing a new breed like the "Salvation Army" onto the streets.

You will feel challenged and inspired to take risks and realize that the Great Commission can actually be an exciting journey! Seeking the lost is not a method but an interactive partnership with the Holy Spirit as He breaks your heart for the lost. Kevin is lighting a fire for the end-time harvest, bringing in a whole new wineskin to the Body of Christ.

Jill Austin
Founder/President of Master Potter Ministries
Author and conference speaker
www.masterpotter.com
info@masterpotter.com

After reading Kevin's book, the wonder of the treasure hunt increased all the more in my life. I loved the "God stories." I laughed and cried my way through the chapters and found myself in increasing evangelistic encounters after reading the book. Anyone interested in seeing His Kingdom on earth as it is in Heaven will be thrilled with this engaging book.

Dr. Heidi Baker
Founding Director of Iris Ministries
Mozambique

The Ultimate Treasure Hunt is the most exciting book I have ever read on the subject of evangelism. The stories are so faith building. The explanations of why all should be on the treasure hunt and how to go about a treasure hunt are powerful. Realizing that the lost are the treasure and we are the hunters, and that the Holy Spirit will give us the clues to find the treasure, is so refreshing.

I wish I could have read this book over 30 years ago while I was in seminary or even earlier while majoring in religious studies in college. What a difference it makes between going on a treasure hunt led by the Holy Spirit and going out "cold calling." It is like the difference between firing a cruise missile guided by GPS and firing a skud missile hoping it might by accident hit a target. This is a great book on a great subject illustrated with great examples. It is a faith builder. It is what I would expect from a staff member of Bethel Church and an associate of Bill Johnson. Buy it! Read it! Apply it! This book could turn you into an on-fire witness for Christ, a transformed treasure hunter full of joy.

The Ultimate Treasure Hunt will change your view and understanding of evangelism. Kevin Dedmon has written what I believe will become an evangelism classic.

Randy Clark
Global Awakening Ministries

Contents

Foreword

❦

WHEN I FIRST BEGAN TO READ the manuscript for *The Ultimate Treasure Hunt*, I thought I knew a little about what to expect. Kevin Dedmon and his family moved here to be a part of our school of ministry a number of years ago. He had already been recognized by two very good organizations as a successful pastor, but was hungry for something more. It takes true humility for a seasoned pastor to sit alongside a new believer in a ministry school that trains people in a signs and wonders lifestyle. No matter how it may have appeared to others, he and his family came to learn. Desperation and humility often work in tandem to bring us into our God-ordained destinies.

Kevin moved from the *idea* of displaying God's power to the *actual experience*. His application of the truths taught made him stand out in a most remarkable way. It didn't take long to recognize that Kevin had an unusually strong anointing for evangelism. We asked both him and his wife, Theresa, to join our pastoral team.

I watched as his whole family took on a lifestyle of risk. The results of pursuing God's purpose for their lives are quite amazing, and some are mentioned in this book. His message and lifestyle bring others into a similar break-through.

Many believers dismiss their responsibility in leading others to Christ by stating, "I don't have a gift for evangelism." Kevin brings both evangelism and the gifts of the Spirit into such a beautiful union that no one is left with a viable excuse. As a result of their ministry, churches and church leaders all across the country are experiencing similar miracles, even after Kevin and our students leave town. That is the exciting thing to me: The miracles are not dependent on an individual, but are a way of life that the Holy Spirit makes available to everyone. God is the extravagant One. Our job is to create a place for Him to invade.

As I read through this manuscript, I discovered what I expected to be there: stories and teaching that make miracles a normal part of the Christian life. Yet, I was also pleasantly surprised. I didn't expect to have tears come to my eyes. Nor did I expect to laugh out loud. I quickly became excited, realizing that in a short period of time this book would be put into the hands of hungry people who would become equipped to make a difference in the world around them.

So, it is with great pleasure I commend to you both the man and the message, for they are one and the same. Welcome to *The Ultimate Treasure Hunt.*

Bill Johnson
Senior Pastor, Bethel Church
Redding, California

Introduction

⚜️

THE *ULTIMATE TREASURE HUNT* is about supernatural encounters. It is about learning to live a naturally supernatural Kingdom lifestyle, in which miracles, physical healing, the prophetic, and setting people free are normal occurrences, as we release the presence and power of the Kingdom of God to the people we know and meet every day.

God wants us to *have* an encounter, so that we *become* an encounter, so that *others* can have an encounter. It is only as we encounter His presence in profound ways that we become a habitation of His presence, so that wherever we go, we naturally *leak* what is inside of us, so that the environment around us is affected by His presence within us.

The Ultimate Treasure Hunt is about supernatural evangelism. It is about having supernatural encounters with the people whom the Father has already prepared for a divine appointment, and that the Holy Spirit will guide us toward, in order to reveal the truth of Jesus Christ. What leads people to repentance is the kindness of God, demonstrated through His people healing the sick, prophesying the secrets of people's hearts, revealing their true destiny, and setting people free to live a blessed life.

The Ultimate Treasure Hunt is about equipping, empowering, and activating the believer to live a naturally supernatural lifestyle of supernatural evangelism. The aim is to increase the level of confidence and competence, so that every believer is able to take responsibility in being the "witness" Jesus has commanded.

This book is *not* intended for those who have the gift of evangelism. In fact, this book is designed for those who feel very intimidated and insecure when it comes to witnessing and evangelism. I hope those who shirk the most at the thought of doing evangelism will find this book refreshing and helpful.

On the other hand, I pray that many will find that they are much more gifted than they previously thought, once they are equipped and empowered through the testimonies and principles taught in each chapter. These testimonies and principles, however, can only be activated through risk. At some point, you will have to step out and *do* the Treasure Hunt, in order to gain the impartations that are available in each chapter. And when you do, you will find, as I have, that you have what it takes to be a naturally supernatural Christian.

This is *not* a book about "street witnessing." In fact, I do not particularly like the term street witnessing because it often connotes only targeting the homeless, drug addicts, gang members, and the "down and out" of society. Obviously, God wants us to reach out to these *people groups*, and I do, but He also intends to save the lawyers, doctors, supermarket clerks, delivery drivers, teachers, classmates, business associates, and stay-at-home moms.

God wants to transform a community, not just those on the "streets." Therefore, I never refer to our Christian witness as going to the "streets," but rather, to the "community." *The Ultimate Treasure Hunt* is about demonstrating God's goodness and kindness to everyone, wherever we go.

This book is *not* about *arguing* someone into confessing Christ. It is *not* about coming up with the right answers to convince someone to agree with your particular doctrine. If someone can be talked *into* something, they can also be talked *out of* something.

This Ultimate Treasure Hunt is about bringing the *Good News* of the Kingdom to every kind of person through supernatural means and demonstration, through supernatural encounters. If you apply the principles of this book, you will see an increase in divine appointments and divine encounters in your everyday life. As you step out and take risk, you will find countless, undreamed of Treasures that will cause incredible rejoicing on earth and in Heaven.

Happy Treasure Hunting!

CHAPTER 1

The Ultimate Treasure

W̲E FOLLOWED OUR TREASURE MAP, which led us to Wal-Mart on our journey to find the ultimate treasure. We did not know exactly what we were going to find, because the only clues we had were headache, blue shirt, Starbucks coffee, knee pain, hurt right arm, frozen foods, red hat, CDs, and bucket. As we headed into the store, our Treasure Hunting team shared some nervous thoughts about whether or not we would actually find the treasure that was hidden somewhere inside. Since I was the only experienced Treasure Hunter on our team of four, I shared that I, too, was always nervous before a big hunt, but that God had always led me to the treasure in the past.

We began to weave our way through the aisles, looking intently in every direction for the subtle clues that would lead us to specific treasures just waiting to be discovered. We made our way over to the frozen food section, where one of the clues on the Treasure Map directed us, but as we stood there, trying to discern every possible lead, it was apparent that our treasure was not in the frozen food section. Knowing that God does not hide things *from* us, but *for* us, I encouraged the team to look beyond the frozen foods.

Immediately, a young woman on the team exclaimed that a young boy being pushed in a cart down a perpendicular aisle had on a blue shirt! With adrenaline pumping through seemingly every muscle in our bodies, as subtly as possible, we approached the treasure site to uncover any treasure that might be hidden for us in a blue shirt. We approached the young boy who was being guarded by his obviously distraught mother.

With smiles on our faces, we explained that we were on a Treasure Hunt, and that we had a blue shirt on our Treasure Map. The mother was visibly skeptical, looking at each of us for signs of an impending scam. But as the mother quizzically scanned our lists highlighting the various clues, she hesitantly pointed out that her son had constant headaches caused by an unidentifiable disease that was affecting his central nervous system. Over the past six months, this young boy had been suffering from incapacitating headaches that had left him virtually crippled.

We explained to the mom that God had led us to them to help them in some way, that they were the Treasure on our map. The mother began to cry, explaining to us that she had been so tired and hopeless as a single mother trying to care for her pain-riddled son. Even though she was not a Christian, she readily welcomed our prayers for her and her son. So, right there in the aisle, we invited God's presence as we laid hands on the little boy. After a few minutes, he began to feel much better, so we began to prophesy Heaven's destiny over mom and son. By the end of the ten-minute encounter, we were all like family, hugging and rejoicing together. The mom then gave her phone number to a woman on our team, asking if she could go to church!

We were so excited about the divine appointment that we had just had, that we could not wait to find the next treasure on our Map. So, we went looking for Starbucks coffee. We went to the raw coffee-bean section, but did not discover our treasure there. Immediately, we were struck once again that we had just "lucked" out somehow with the divine appointment with the "blue shirt" and the "headache."

I instructed the team that we often need to dig deeper for the clues, that creativity is a big part of successful Treasure Hunting. We began to think of all of the different places that Starbucks coffee would be located in the store, and discovered that there were two other locations. We went to the ground-coffee section, and finding no further clues there, we went to the ice cream section where, unbeknownst to me, they had frozen Starbucks ice cream!

As we stood there, we realized that earlier we had "frozen foods" and that now we were in the frozen section different from what we had previously deduced from that clue on our Treasure Map. We waited in the empty aisle for about three minutes, now knowing that this was the place where we would find our next treasure.

Finally, a woman who was an acquaintance of one of our team members came walking down our aisle. We explained that we were on a Treasure Hunt and that we were looking for further clues. As she looked at our Treasure Map, she could hardly believe that we had "hurt right arm" on our Treasure Map. It turned out that she had hurt her arm several months earlier, and it had still not healed. We began to pray simply, "Lord, let Your Kingdom come; let Your will be done in this arm as it is in Heaven." Immediately, the pain left her arm, and the mobility was fully restored!

So now we're looking for buckets. We headed over to the mops and stood around the buckets there for a few minutes, and then to the automotive section to find a bucket used to wash cars. Nothing. Someone then had the idea that we could go to the toy section where they might have buckets used to play in the sand.

As we were wandering around the toy section looking for a bucket, one of the employees approached me and asked if I needed help. I said, "Well, we're on a Treasure Hunt and one of our clues is a bucket." Trying to be very helpful, she asked why we needed a bucket. "Well," I said, "we actually do not want a bucket; we are looking for a person that God wants to help today who is standing by a bucket—that is our treasure." Sheepishly, she asked, "Do you think I could be your treasure?" Without hesitation, the team began to prophesy over her, calling out the good plans and purposes that God had in store for her. We began to speak about the way God the Father saw her: as the apple of His eye.

Right there in the middle of the aisle, at the buckets, she started crying and sharing with us that everything we said was exactly what she needed to hear. She invited Jesus into her heart and told us that it was the best day of her life!

As she left, we were ecstatic. "This Treasure Hunt thing really works," we were all thinking. Just then, another employee walked by limping, which of course was caused by a problem in his "right knee." Now the Treasures were coming to us! We ended up praying for him, and God healed him right there on the spot. We encouraged him that he had just experienced the goodness and kindness of God and sent him on his way back to work.

We ended up finding the other clues on our Treasure Map, but the most important part of our adventurous journey was that we found the Ultimate Treasure: people who had been buried in loneliness, pain, and hopelessness who, when uncovered by the Holy Spirit's leading, were saved, healed, and delivered all in a time span of a mere 1 hour and 15 minutes!

THERE IS TREASURE EVERYWHERE

The Ultimate Treasure is the people who are just waiting to be discovered. They are those who desperately, and often secretly, need a real encounter with God in order to meet the overwhelming needs of their lives and the unfulfilled desires of their hearts. They are everywhere. They are in stores, businesses, neighborhoods, parks, schools, and even the church. They are everywhere we go. They are God's Ultimate Treasure.

In Luke 15:8-10, Jesus tells a parable that captures God's heart for the lost treasure. He says:

> *Or suppose a woman has ten silver coins and loses one. Does she not light a lamp, sweep the house and search carefully until she finds it? And when she finds it, she calls her friends and neighbors together and says, "Rejoice with me; I have found my lost coin [treasure]." In the same way, I tell you, there is rejoicing in the presence of*

the angels of God over one sinner who repents (Luke 15:8-10).

Too often, we as Christians can look at the "lost coins" in the world as worthless, instead of viewing them as the treasure depicted in this parable. So very easy it is to think of the "sinner" as a lost cause, and therefore, not even worth seeking. It is true that those who are covered over in darkness are under every kind of evil, and that the god of this age has darkened their understanding (see Eph. 4:17), but that should not be the deterrent to uncovering the treasure that lies within them. Everyone is worth finding.

I love how the apostle Paul describes this truth in Ephesians 2:1-5.

> *As for you, you were dead in your transgressions and sins, in which you used to live when you followed the ways of this world and of the ruler of the kingdom of the air, the spirit who is now at work in those who are disobedient. All of us also lived among them at one time, gratifying the cravings of our sinful nature and following its desires and thoughts. Like the rest, we were by nature objects of wrath. But because of His great love for us, God, who is rich in mercy, made us alive with Christ even when we were dead in transgressions—it is by grace you have been saved.*

The apostle Paul certainly knew this revelation from personal experience. In the Book of Acts, we find him leading the charge to persecute the Church. In fact, in First Timothy 1:15, he confesses that, "Christ Jesus came into the world to save sinners—of whom I am the worst." The apostle Paul was an unlikely candidate for the Church's "outreach" program; but nevertheless, Jesus searched him out on the road to Damascus, and Saul became the apostle Paul—the Ultimate Treasure. (See Acts 9.)

A Treasure Worth Finding

I am glad my grandmother and cousin did not see me as a lost cause before I became a Christian as a 16-year-old. My grandfather, who had been a deacon in the Baptist church forever, had just passed away, so my cousin had gone to take care of my grandmother in southern California. That summer, I decided to spend my vacation with them so that I could spend time at the beach and "party" in unending fashion. What I had not realized was that, thanks to Grandma's influence, my cousin had become a Christian.

At 16, I was fully into all that the world had to offer a teenager at that time. A drug-using, rock-and-roll drummer, I was so far away from Christ that I was the last person any of my friends would think could become a Christian. I would come home from the beach, eat every available food item in the house, and constantly mock the Christian television shows they would incessantly watch throughout the evening.

But it was my grandmother's unconditional acceptance of me even with all of my "sinful" baggage, and my cousin's convincing argument that I could go to church with him just as I was that made all the difference. That church happened to be Calvary Chapel in Costa Mesa, California, at the height of the Jesus Movement.

It was 1975, and I showed up to a Saturday night concert high on drugs and expecting to hear organ music and find "dorks" in short-sleeved white shirts with ties. What I found, however, was 2,000 people who were just like me on the outside, but on the inside they had found something that I had not even been looking for, but found that night. No one judged me; I did not need to be judged because I already knew what was wrong with me. What I did not know was what was right with me—that God had a plan for me. Every lyric of every song seemed to have been written for me, expressing my heart's desire for intimacy and significance.

As the preacher got up to give the altar call, I sat there contemplating the choice I was about to make. I knew that following Christ meant giving up all of my sinful practices (crutches), which had not really helped anyway but, being all I knew, seemed better than nothing. I knew I would also need to give up my "friends" even though I often felt agonizing loneliness even in their company. I knew that I needed help for my frequent suicidal thoughts brought on by the gnawing emptiness I felt every day.

But I just could not take the leap. I was afraid of the unknown and the false perception that I had of the Church, and therefore, Christianity. I sat there through two altar calls in which a couple of hundred "wanna be" treasures went forward to be discovered. The preacher began to pray for those who had come forward as I sat lower in my seat next to my cousin who was fervently praying for me under his breath.

Then the minister stopped. He apologized for stopping at such a crucial moment, but he felt like there was just one more person who needed to respond to God's love that night. He briefly said once again that God had a special plan for this person's life, and that if he or she just came forward, that person's life would never be the same, that he or she would experience love and freedom that would satisfy every need and desire.

Immediately, my heart began to race at 8,000 RPMs. I knew he was talking to me. I had never felt so much love and purpose. You see, my high school counselor had just told me that I should think about preparing to get hired on at the city's sanitation department because I would always have steady work there with benefits. I went away thinking that being a garbage collector was appropriate since I thought I was junk anyway.

So, when I heard this preacher calling out my destiny to have significance and live a life full of the love of God, I was overwhelmed. I felt an invisible hand pick me up by the back of the collar of my T-shirt, and the next thing I knew I was running to the front of the church accompanied by the exuberant applause of 2,000 amazed believers! I was the Ultimate Treasure that night.

I was an unlikely coin to have had that much effort employed to find it. In my mind, I was worth about as much as a scuffed up old penny that someone would gladly throw into a "wishing well," aware that the gesture was in vain, but relieved to be rid of the little nuisance in his pocket. It felt strange to me that God not only knew me, but also cared enough about finding me that He would have a preacher stop in the middle of his prayer and highlight me out of 2,000 people.

I felt like a treasure that night, realizing that God does not make junk. I was like the lost coin in the parable. I was so valuable to God that He put all of His focus on finding me. He orchestrated search teams like my grandmother and cousin, who relentlessly wooed me out of the dark hole that I was lost in.

Looking back, I know there were many others who had gone out of their way to shine a search light in my direction, pointing the way to the truth. I do not know any of their names, nor would I likely recognize any of them if I met them face-to-face today. But one day, when we all meet in Heaven to revel in the great Treasure Hunting adventures that we pursued in this world in search of lost coins, I have a feeling that there will be a crowd of those who contributed to the Treasure Hunt to find me.

CELEBRATING DISCOVERED TREASURE

No other place in Scripture depicts all of the angels "rejoicing" than here, in the parable of the lost coin. I guess if all of Heaven is that excited over a Treasure Hunt, it must be a pretty important event in the Kingdom of God. Jesus paid a great price, spending Himself on purchasing these coins. Therefore, just as you would spare no resource searching for a "collectable;" so in locating one person you would go to all lengths. And our Father in Heaven will celebrate their return, just as the father who found his son in Luke 15:24 proclaimed, "He was lost and is found."

I'll never forget my feeling of utter despair when I received the news of our 16-year-old son, Chad, who was 3,000 miles away at a youth conference. We had been dealing with several challenges as a result of the poor lifestyle choices that he had been making. As a pastor, I just assumed that he would grow up as a "Christian," but I had come to realize that he needed to be saved just like I did.

Somehow, unconsciously, I had this thought that he would be the first sinless son since Jesus. I was crushed when I found out that he had been selling drugs out of our home while he was babysitting his 5-year-old sister when we were on our date nights!

We had been working through all of the issues stemming from and contributing to his lifestyle for about a year and a half, when we finally decided that he just needed a personal encounter with God. All of the counseling, the books we read, the talks we had, boundaries we made, and the prayers we prayed were good, but what he needed most was a *divine appointment* in which he heard God for himself.

So, we sent him off across the country with a youth group from another church to attend a national youth conference. We prayed. The youth leaders had told us that if our son, who did not really want to go, caused any problems, he would be sent home on the first available flight. So with fear and trepidation, we sent him off, hoping that the treasure inside of him would get discovered.

I was in my office two days after the five-day conference had started when the phone rang. It was my wife, crying uncontrollably. All she could manage to get out was, "It's Chad; it's Chad." Immediately, I was thinking, *Oh great, he's got into trouble, and they are sending him home.* My heart sunk down to the floor. After a few minutes, my wife gained enough composure to explain to me that she had received a phone call from the youth pastor. He reported to her that our son had been crying for the first 24 hours of the conference, confessing his sin and repenting. He went on to say that he had spent the next 24 hours laughing hysterically.

Of course, by now I was picking up my proud pumping heart off the floor where it had been lying for the previous painstaking five minutes. My first thought was, *My son was lost, and now he's found!* Now, ten years later, my son and daughter-in-love are on the pastoral staff of a large church in southern California. Not many days go by without my still rejoicing over the day my treasured son was found.

WITNESSING IS **NOT** A GIFT

Of course, God has been into Treasure Hunting since the first coin was lost in the Garden of Eden. Throughout the Old Testament, beginning with the first glimpse of the gospel in Genesis 3:15 in which God promised that even though satan would strike man's heel, man would crush satan's head, we find God's redemptive plans unfolding to recover that which had been lost. God spent a long time, over 4,000 years, looking for just the right time and place to reveal the secrets of the lost treasure. It only makes sense, then, that He and all of Heaven would be ecstatic with joy as the long lost treasure is dug up out of the dark pit of destruction and death.

Jesus' whole mission was to "seek and save what was lost" (Luke 19:10). He then told His disciples to "go, and make disciples of all nations." The word "nations" is the Greek word *ethnos,* from which we get the word "ethnic." It has the connotation of a people group with specific distinctives. In a sense, Jesus was telling His disciples to go to every social group. So many of us can get into the trap of thinking that witnessing is something that we do on the "streets" to homeless people. But the homeless make up just one of the many "*ethnos*" groups of the world.

Lost treasures are just waiting to be found in every segment of every society. The Book of Acts is a demonstration of God's heart of "not wanting anyone to perish, but everyone to come to repentance" (2 Pet. 3:9). We find throughout the Book of Acts example after example of those being saved from every sphere of society: governors, jail guards, religious terrorists, practitioners of witchcraft, the rich, the poor, servants, and masters are all discovered treasures.

Each one of us is a treasure to God. He bought each one of us with a price: the precious blood of Jesus. And when we are finally found, there is rejoicing because collectively and individually we are His Ultimate Treasure!

Obviously then, if God's heart is to find His lost treasure, then having His heart, we would have the same passion and resolve to look in every "nook and cranny" to find the treasures waiting to be discovered around us. To be a Treasure Hunter does not take a special gift, but it does take the Father's heart of compassion to care enough about what is lost to do something about finding it.

Many have the false understanding that because they do not have the "gift" of an evangelist, they do not have the responsibility or the capacity to witness. Timothy, however, was instructed by the apostle Paul "to do the work of an evangelist" even though he was a pastor/teacher type. The "apostle" Paul, himself, was not an "evangelist," yet he led many to Christ through his witness.

While evangelism can be a gift, the Bible is clear that "witnessing" is not a gift, but a responsibility. Jesus commanded the disciples in Acts 1:8, "You will be My witnesses...." Clearly, there were those among the disciples who were more outgoing than others, and maybe even had a "gift" (although we are not told); nevertheless, they were all commanded to witness. They were all called to be Treasure Hunters, searching for the Ultimate Treasure.

CHAPTER 2

The Ultimate Treasure Hunter

＊＊＊＊＊

ONE OF MY FAVORITE MOVIES is the Indiana Jones' movie: *Raiders of the Lost Ark*. For some reason, I'm drawn vicariously into every scene as though I could actually be Indiana Jones in a jungle, hunting down the ultimate treasure. As I watch those fictitious, extreme adventures of risk, something rises up within me that just makes me want to go after the great treasures that are hidden for me to find.

Unfortunately, however, for too many Christians, reading the Bible is kind of like watching an Indiana Jones movie. It is so easy to read page after page and story after story of heroes who risked everything, cheering on their success, while at the same time, feeling incapacitated to enter into the adventure ourselves.

One of my greatest heroes in the Bible is Ananias. I'm not referring to the Ananias of Acts chapter 5 who was married to Sapphira and who died when he lied about part of an offering that he never actually gave. That Ananias was not resurrected. The Ananias that I am referring to is the man found in Acts chapter 9. He is the Ultimate Treasure Hunter. He is my hero.

You are probably very familiar with the events of Acts chapter 9 in which Saul, later known as the apostle Paul, had a miraculous encounter with Jesus on the road to Damascus. Most of us stop there in communicating the story. What we can easily overlook is that without Ananias, the Ultimate Treasure Hunter, there would not have been the apostle Paul, the Ultimate Treasure.

Ananias stands out to me because he was just an ordinary guy. He was not an apostle. He was not a deacon. He was not on the church "ministry team" as far as we know. Ananias most likely was not an evangelist. If anything, he was more of a worshiping intercessor, for we find him in prayer when Jesus shows up in a vision to reveal the clues for a supernatural Treasure Hunt. Ananias was the least likely candidate as the Ultimate Treasure Hunter. He is just like many of us who feel insecure and incompetent about leading people to Christ.

Many people have an idea that in order to do the work of evangelism, one must be extroverted and well-trained in answering every possible question that might arise in a given encounter. But as far as we know, Ananias was not an extrovert, and if he was a scholar, it is not highlighted as important to the Treasure Hunt.

Ananias was just hanging out with God in the "secret place," in the place of intimacy, maybe even diligently praying for worldwide revival as commanded by Jesus in Acts 1:8: "You shall be My witnesses in Jerusalem, Judea, Samaria, and to the ends of the earth." And it was in this context of intimate prayer that Jesus appeared to Ananias in Acts chapter 9. "Yes, Lord," he answered in verse 10.

OBEYING THE DIRECTIONS

The best Treasure Hunters are those who not only learn to hear the voice of the Lord in the secret place of prayer, but also those who obey the directions they get in the secret place who ultimately find the Ultimate Treasures. In Acts 1:11, the next verse, Jesus tells Ananias to "Go." The Church has spent enough time in the "prayer closet." It is time to do what Jesus commanded us to do—to go!

My wife, Theresa, who is an incredible Treasure Hunter, was in prayer one morning when the Holy Spirit spoke to her about going to a certain local supermarket to find some Treasure before coming to our weekly pastors' staff meeting. She was running a little late that morning but decided to follow the prompting she had received. She walked into the store with "produce" and "grief" as her only clues.

As she stood there in the produce section, she began to evaluate all of the potential Treasure. After five minutes or so, feeling a little bewildered that no one seemed to fit the description, she noticed a woman standing by the corn. Motionless, and looking blankly into space, she appeared distraught as she stood with her cart.

Theresa approached her and explained to her about the Treasure Hunt she was on. She went on to ask whether the woman was dealing with any grief issues because of the "grief" clue she had received. The woman broke into tears, explaining how she had just recently lost her husband to cancer, and how that just a few days prior, their dog had died. She had barely slept since and had not eaten anything. Through her tears, she explained that even though she was severely depressed, she felt like she needed to go to the store. Once she got to the produce department, however, she had no idea why she was there.

After empathetically listening to the woman's story, Theresa offered to pray with her. The woman agreed, and Theresa began praying prophetic prayers of hope and comfort. After she had finished, the woman looked up at her, wiped away the tears, and asked, "Are you an angel?"

Theresa is an Ultimate Treasure Hunter because she has learned to go when she hears something in the prayer closet. She was not always like that. When I met her 30 years ago, she was fairly shy and cautious around strangers. Doing something like she did that day at the supermarket would have been unthinkable. But over the years, she has become an Ultimate Treasure Hunter all because she has been willing to go.

In Matthew chapter 10, Jesus sent out the 12 disciples telling them to "Go" (v. 6). In Luke chapter 10, Jesus sent out the 72, telling them once again to "Go!" (v.3). In Matthew chapter 28, and again in Acts 1:8, Jesus commands His disciples to "Go!" By now, we are getting the point, right? "Go!"

BREAKING THROUGH FEAR

So here is Ananias, an introverted intercessor, and in a vision, Jesus shows up in the prayer meeting! He has a simple message: "Go...." In the following verses, He begins to download specific instructions for the Ultimate Treasure Hunt—clues that Ananias could have never known apart from divine revelation.

> *Go to the house of Judas on Straight Street and ask for a man from Tarsus named Saul, for he is praying. In a vision he has seen a man named Ananias come and place his hands on him to restore his sight* (Acts 9:11).

Most of us, if we had an encounter like this, would be filled with the confidence and boldness to immediately go out and fulfill the Lord's request. Wrong. Look at Ananias' faith-filled response in the next verse.

> *"Lord...I have heard many reports about this man and all the harm he has done to your saints in Jerusalem. And he has come here with authority from the chief priests to arrest all who call on Your name"* (Acts 9:13-14).

Ananias' response here represents that of many Christians I encounter when challenging them to "go" as Jesus commanded. The normal reaction to the call to witness is generally one of fear. "They are going to reject me, persecute me, or even kill me." "I do not have what it takes." "I'm not gifted" are just some of the excuses we use to put off the Treasure Hunt.

Notice that Jesus does not respond to Ananias' fear. Kris Vallotton, our senior associate pastor on staff, often challenges us that "The dogs of doom are always standing at the doorway of our destiny." Moreover, the thing we fear the most is oftentimes the doorway into our destiny. God did not give us a spirit of timidity (fear), but a spirit of power, of love, and of self-discipline (2 Tim. 1:7). So, here is Ananias, afraid to "go." There is only one way to break through the fear: to "go," which is Jesus' instruction in the following verses.

> "...Go! This man is My chosen instrument to carry My name before the Gentiles and their kings and before the people of Israel. I will show him how much he must suffer for My name" (Acts 9:15-16).

Notice that Jesus does not capitulate to Ananias' hesitancy to go. He does not respond the way we would to so many today in the Church. He does not give in to Ananias' fear saying, "I know that you are not an evangelist, Ananias. I know that you are afraid, lack confidence, and feel incompetent. Do not worry, I will find someone else to go on the Treasure Hunt."

No, Jesus simply tells him again to "Go!" although this time it is with the exclamation point. In other words, like my mother used to warn, "Don't make me have to tell you again." Amazingly, it took about eight years before the apostles finally ventured out of Jerusalem to fulfill the command of Acts 1:8, to be "witnesses in Jerusalem, and in all Judea and Samaria, and the ends of the earth." It was persecution that ultimately led them into the "faith" to leave Jerusalem to fulfill that call to "go."

By Acts chapter 9, maybe Ananias had learned enough through experience that *not* going was not an option. We obviously do not know what he was thinking at that moment, but what we do know is that he went, following the clues and finding the Ultimate Treasure in a guy named Saul, whom we now know as the great apostle Paul. Ananias was not the Ultimate Treasure Hunter because he was the most gifted, but simply because he was willing to go. He broke through his fear, and entered into his destiny as a Treasure Hunter.

A TRANSFORMED TREASURE HUNTER

I was in Miami, Florida, empowering and activating a church to be Treasure Hunters. When it came time to go out and find the Treasure, one of the key leaders became visibly anxious. Having seen this time and again, especially with church leaders, I promised him that he could just come along and watch, that he would not have to do anything other than help get the Treasure Map. He reluctantly agreed, expressing that Treasure Hunting was not his calling and that he did not feel comfortable "pushing religion down people's throats." Because he was so skeptical and was an influential leader in the church, I decided to take him in my group.

Soon after, we all got our Treasure Maps and began to get a fix on the locations in which we had clues. The skeptical, "non-gifted" leader hesitantly handed his map over to correlate with the others. He had several clues like "blue jeans," "post office box," "blue truck," "knee problems," "James," "black man," "glasses," and "salvation."

We hopped in a car and made our way over to a large strip mall. We had been on the Treasure Hunt about an hour when we realized not one of the skeptical leader's clues had been found. We had already found several people on the list, including seeing one guy healed of a wrist injury at the "shovels" in a "hardware" section of a "home improvement store." As the leader watched the man give his life to Christ right there in the store, he began to show a little excitement. Amazingly, this leader had never been a part of leading anyone to Christ in public.

After seeing such a pronounced demonstration of the Kingdom of God, he began to intently check his list, looking up every few moments, scouring the strip mall for any signs of the clues on *his* Treasure Map. I could see the anticipation growing inside of him as we searched out several dead-end leads.

As we were walking back to our car, feeling a little bad for not having found any of the clues on the skeptic's list, he shouted out that he saw a "post office mail box" in front of one of the stores that had previously gone unnoticed by our team. He further exclaimed that a "blue truck" was parked right in front of it.

The leader ran to the Treasure Hunting site he had located, leaving us behind. When we caught up with him, he was breathing hard and sweating profusely, but not because of the short run, rather, because he just knew he was going to find some precious Treasure.

We waited for about five minutes, standing by the "mail box" and the "blue truck" without any Treasure in sight. I tried to encourage him, explaining that sometimes we get clues that do not lead to Treasure, but that God is just as pleased with us for "going." But he would have none of it. A spirit of confidence came over him that convinced all of us to stay a little longer. This skeptical leader had turned into a faith-filled, fireball evangelist because he had found two clues on his Treasure Map.

Moments later, several construction workers came out of a restaurant next to where we had been standing. They were followed by a large "black man," wearing "blue jeans," and "glasses." Every step he took was slow and laborious. He was in obvious pain as he made his way over to the truck where his crew was waiting.

The transformed leader in our Treasure Hunting group wasted no time "accosting" the potential Treasure. It turned out that the man had agonizing pain in his "knees" caused by arthritis. And of course his name was "James." After building some nervous rapport, the leader asked if the man would like to feel better. "Of course," he replied. The leader went on to say how we had just prayed for others that very day who had been miraculously healed. He then asked if James would like us to pray for him like we had prayed for the others.

James was not a Christian, but he was desperate. So, with his crew looking on, we gathered around him and prayed. The leader prayed a simple prayer, and in a matter of moments, the man was completely healed. He started jumping up and down, and then bending up and down to demonstrate what he could not do a few moments prior. The on-looking crew began to cheer from the back of the truck, prompting a few of our team to begin to share with them about God's good purposes for their lives, a message met with full receptivity.

Just then, two women pulled up in a car and parked beside the truck where we were speaking with James. One of the ladies was his wife, who had been praying for her husband, James, for many years. When she found out that he had just been healed, she broke into tears and proclaimed,

"Thank You, Jesus. I knew You could get James." So right there in the parking lot, standing next to the blue truck, next to the "mailbox," the church leader led James to Christ ("salvation").

When we got back to the church to share testimonies with the other Treasure Hunters who had gone out to find Treasure like we had found, we could not hold back the formerly skeptical leader once it came time to share. He recounted every detail of the Treasure Hunt leading up to his divine appointment with James. He confidently concluded with the declaration that he was going to be a Treasure Hunter the rest of his life.

That day, this leader found that Treasure Hunting is not about "shoving religion down people's throats" but demonstrating the goodness and kindness of God, as the Scriptures confirm, "It is the kindness of God that leads us to repentance" (Rom.2:4). He found that when the Kingdom of God is released through the supernatural, the "Good News" is truly good news, and that just like on the Day of Pentecost, the desired response by the recipients is "...what shall we do *to be saved?*" (Acts 2:37).

A classic example of this approach is Jesus' encounter with the woman at the well in the Gospel of John, chapter 4. Jesus had just sent His disciples off to get some lunch. While He was waiting at the well for their return, a Samaritan woman came to draw water. Jesus, being thirsty, asked the woman to dip some water out for Him. But the woman recognized that He was a Jew and began to challenge His cultural literacy, for Jews did not associate with Samaritans in those days.

Jesus, however, began to describe the living water that He could give to her in return. In a sense, He was attempting to make her thirsty. But the message itself was apparently not enough to convince her of the true identity of Jesus. So then He shared inside information about her life that no one could have known, but God, in order to reveal His deity.

In an attempt to deflect the truth, she launched into a theological debate, which Jesus countered by revealing Himself to her. The scene ended with the woman leaving her water pot and running back into town to invite others to come see the Christ, Jesus. The Jews and Samaritans had been arguing for some 500 years over theology. Not until a woman at a well had a personal encounter with Jesus, accentuated by the "word of knowledge" revealing the secrets of her life, were she and many other Samaritans won over.

UNCOVERING TREASURES THROUGH ENCOUNTERS

I believe many Christians shy away from witnessing because the only models they have seen are either very invasive or argumentative. How many of us enjoy being accosted with the salesman's pitch to get us to buy something we do not need or want? Unfortunately, many Christians are perceived with the same disdain as the unwanted salesman. How many of us cringe listening to the futile, fruitless arguments in the lunchroom in the name of "witnessing." As a result, many shy away from witnessing to avoid leaving a "bad taste" in the non-Christian's mouth to protect the reputation of the Church.

Of course, the apostle Peter instructs us in First Peter 3:15 to "Always be prepared to give an answer to everyone who asks you to give the reason for the hope that you have. But do this with gentleness and respect...." Some read this passage and assume that Peter is speaking about giving an intellectual reason for the hope, that he wants us to prepare a theological dissertation for the existence of God that would convince even the most hardened atheist.

I have rarely ever led someone to Christ through argument. Not because I cannot argue, but because at some point the debate requires a leap of faith, "It is by grace you are saved, through faith" (Eph. 2:8), not debate. Obviously, a debate can lead someone to the point of deciding to take the leap.

Billy Graham is a classic example of someone who is masterful at walking a crowd through the logical steps toward the launching pad of faith. But most people do not come into the Kingdom through a well-developed argument. They come through an encounter, whether it is a personal testimony of how someone else encountered God in some way, or a supernatural encounter in which God revealed Himself to them in a specific way.

The reality is a man with an experience is never at the mercy of a man with an argument. And a man with an argument is only one encounter away from changing his argument! The apostle Paul had a pretty good argument that Christians should be persecuted. He spent all of his time and resources toward that end. Yet on the road to Damascus, when Jesus appeared to him personally, he was ready to change his argument. When Ananias showed up a few days later by divine appointment, Paul gladly accepted the counter message of the good news and spent the rest of his life promoting it wherever he went.

AN ANGEL REVEALS THE TREASURE

Recently, my son Chad took a group of junior high school kids out Treasure Hunting. They had several odd clues that led them to the parking lot of a well-known supermarket. One of the kids had "a woman with a back injury" on his list. As my son scanned across the parking lot, he saw an angel holding a banner that read "encounter" over a Middle Eastern woman who was beside her van.

Chad and the team approached the woman and asked if she wanted prayer. The woman adamantly declined, indicating that she was in a hurry. Instantly, the "back injury" clue came to his mind as the woman was backing out of the parking space, and he yelled out, "You were in a car accident two weeks ago. You have pain in your back and it hurts to sit down." Absolutely shocked, she stopped in the middle of the parking lot and confessed that she had been in a severe car accident two weeks prior, leaving her with a debilitating back injury.

They began to explain to the woman that they were on a Treasure Hunt and that she was the Treasure they were looking for. Chad then explained about the angel that he had just seen over her, and then felt impressed to boldly tell her that Jesus had recently visited her in her dreams. The woman began to cry and explained that she had been a very dedicated Muslim her whole life, but had recently been visited by Jesus four times over the previous ten nights in her dreams. She had not known what to make of the visitations other than that the messages she had received specifically told her to be expecting an "encounter."

Chad and the team gathered around and began to release the presence of Jesus on the Muslim woman.

Immediately, all of the pain left her back, and she was completely healed. Chad then talked to her about Jesus, and she responded, "I want to know Jesus the way you know Jesus."

So, there in a parking lot, this Muslim woman had an encounter that changed her theology in a moment. The team did not argue with her about the differences between Islam and Christianity. No, they just demonstrated the Kingdom of God in response to some "clues" they had received from the Holy Spirit, and followed a vision that directed them to the place in which God had already prepared a treasured heart to receive Him.

JESUS PREPARES THE WAY

When Ananias showed up at Saul's house with his Treasure Map, little did he know that God had already prepared Saul's heart as well. (See Acts 9.) We are told that after Saul saw the light and heard Jesus' voice on the road to Damascus, he was blind for three days and did not eat or drink anything. I believe Saul's blindness was symbolic of the lack of revelation he had of Jesus.

In verse 5, Saul responds to Jesus' question, "Why do you persecute Me?" with "Who are You, Lord?" The word "Lord" in the Greek language can also mean "Sir," which I believe to be the correct translation in this case. Obviously, Paul did not know the identity of Jesus, which prompted the question. The revelation comes in the next verse, "I am Jesus, whom you are persecuting."

The point is this: God is preparing people everywhere through visions, dreams, and supernatural encounters. Although they remain blind to the truth, they are, nevertheless, hungry and thirsty for true revelation of God. They are just waiting for an Ananias to come and lay hands on them so they can see. The question remains: Will we go? Will we step out of our comfort zone and become the Ultimate Treasure Hunters that we were all made to be?

CHAPTER 3

The Treasure Map Clues

✦✦✦✦

B Y THIS TIME YOU ARE PROBABLY WONDERING how we get the clues for the Treasure Map. It is actually quite simple. We merely ask the Holy Spirit to give us "words of knowledge," providing clues for the divine appointments where the Treasures are waiting. A "word of knowledge," or "message of knowledge" (in the New International Version) is simply knowing something about something or someone we could not have known without the Holy Spirit telling us.

When the word of knowledge is utilized in witnessing, it creates an undeniable invitation into a divine encounter, which often results in found Treasure. In John chapter 1, when Jesus saw Nathanael approaching, He said of him, "Here is a true Israelite, in whom there is nothing false." When asked how Jesus knew this information, He responded, "I saw you while you were still under the fig tree before Philip called you."

Obviously, Nathanael was keenly aware that only God, or someone who represented God, could have known the specific details of his character and activities. And it was that revelation that prompted him to declare, "Rabbi, You are the Son of God; You are the King of Israel." Interestingly, that simple, yet specific and insightful word of knowledge led to Nathanael's becoming one of the 12 disciples—even though he originally was the ultimate skeptic before he met Jesus as seen when he asked, "Nazareth! Can anything good come from there?" (See John 1:46-49.)

It only makes sense that if Jesus utilized this gift to find Treasure, then we would want to ask the Holy Spirit to give us every advantage available in succeeding in finding the Treasures we are looking for. Sure, you can find Treasure without inside information, but why senselessly search through the soil when a spiritual metal detector is available? The "word of knowledge" is an effective resource, accessible to every believer, to accomplish the task of finding the Ultimate Treasures and fulfilling the Great Commission.

According to First Corinthians 12, this gift, along with the others listed, "is given for the common good." In other words, having inside information about something or someone is supposed to be good for everyone. As mentioned in the previous chapter, Jesus had a "word [message] of knowledge" regarding the Samaritan woman at the well, and it convinced her that she was indeed speaking with the Christ.

Obviously, there are times when people use the gift to hurt others, by revealing their sins to everyone around. Jesus, however, demonstrated honor and respect to the Samaritan woman by keeping her secret between the two of them. Jesus was not interested in exposing her, but redeeming her. Most people already know what is wrong with them. What they do not know is what is *right* about them— what their destiny is in Christ, and the good plans and purposes He has for them.

As I am writing, I can already hear some thinking, *But what about sin? We need to convince them that they are sinners so that they will repent.* I absolutely agree with the need to repent, but many Christians put the proverbial cart before the horse.

On the Day of Pentecost, in Acts chapter 2, the Holy Spirit was poured out on the Church, and 3,000 people were saved that very day. So we would expect Peter to have preached a salvation message imploring the people to repent from their sins. Peter's stellar message, however, was to just explain what had happened—what they had seen demonstrated before their very eyes.

He begins in verse 14 with an explanation for their apparent "drunken" state, in which he uses a passage from the Old Testament Book of Joel to verify that this condition had been prophesied in the Scriptures.

> *In the last days, God says, I will pour out My Spirit on all people. Your sons and daughters will prophesy, your young men will see visions, your old men will dream dreams. Even on My servants, both men and women, I will pour out My Spirit in those days...* (Acts 2:17-18).

Peter then goes on to describe the true identity of Jesus as prophesied by David, and how He was crucified, buried, and raised from the dead in spite of all the odds against Him. The people were so moved by what they saw and by what they had heard that day, that they had only one response, "Brothers, what shall we do?" Only then did Peter instruct them to repent.

Heaven's strategy was to demonstrate the manifest presence of God through the signs and wonders that the people witnessed, then to explain what had just happened, waiting for the right response before asking for a commitment. I believe many non-Christians are negative toward the "Good News" because of our frequent lack of demonstrating the Kingdom we are attempting to promote.

Most of us would never buy a car without test-driving it. Without a demonstration, it is virtually impossible to experience all of the benefits of the car you intend to buy. Interestingly, statistics show that if a customer test-drives a car, he is much more likely to buy it. Similarly, people tend to respond much better to a demonstration of power than a detailed "sales pitch" on the features and benefits of Heaven.

The apostle Paul found this out when he visited Athens in Acts 17. In Athens, he preached one of the most articulate messages in Scripture. Many seminaries study Paul's preaching style in order to better equip promising new preachers who are ready to be unleashed out into the world. What has been overlooked, however, is that at the end of the message, we are told that "only a few men became followers...."

Interestingly, the next place Paul traveled was Corinth in which he later explains to the Church that had been established on that visit that:

My message and my preaching were not with wise and persuasive words, but with a demonstration of the Spirit's power, so that your faith might not rest on men's wisdom, but on God's power (1 Corinthians 2:4-5).

We know from various sources that the church at Corinth had readily received the gospel when Paul preached. According to his account, it was the demonstration that convinced them, not the eloquent message that he had preached in Athens. My pastor, Bill Johnson, says it well when he says, "Without power, the gospel is not good news." This statement is usually followed by this challenge: "We owe the world an encounter." I believe people are hungry for God these days. What they need is a demonstration of the Spirit's power to satisfy their curiosity.

DEMONSTRATION AT HOME DEPOT

I'll never forget the time I was in a Home Depot doing a Treasure Hunt. Among the many clues we had together, on my map, I had "red hair," "headache," "Ralph," and "back problem." We had just finished ministering to a young man, also on our list, wearing a "black hat," and "black and grey sweatshirt," who had "marriage problems." As we were walking away from the checkout stand, I noticed a woman with "red hair" about 30 feet away. As I approached her and her husband, I yelled out, "Hey, do you by any chance have a headache?" to which she responded, "As a matter of fact I do!"

She explained to us that she had just mentioned to her husband that she was going to have to leave their full cart because she had developed a severe migraine headache since coming into the store about an hour prior to meeting us. She was absolutely shocked that I had some inside information that no one could have known. After explaining that God speaks to us and that He had clearly highlighted her, I asked if we could pray for her. She heartily agreed, while her 6'4", 250-pound husband took a few steps back to quietly observe.

In a matter of seconds, the woman reported that she felt heat on the back of her head where I had placed my hand to pray for her. Immediately, her headache vanished and she started to cry, overwhelmed that God would care enough about her to send us to help her. Even though she was not a Christian, she gladly let us pray for her again, and then asked Jesus into her life right there in the middle of Home Depot.

As we were walking away, I realized that I also had the name "Ralph" on my Treasure Map. From about 20 feet away, I yelled back to the husband of the woman who had just been healed, "Hey, I forgot to ask, but by any chance, is your name Ralph?"

"As a matter of fact it is," he responded.

At that, we went back to them to show him the Treasure Map on which his name was located.

Now Ralph had been standing off to the side the entire time we were ministering to his wife. He had appeared very skeptical and was unresponsive to anything that had happened to his wife. But this "word of knowledge" immediately peaked his interest. I began to go down the various clues on our Treasure Maps, and at each ailment, he matter-of-factly denied having them. When I got to "back problem," he did the same, but this time his wife spoke up and said, "Come on, Ralph, you know you cannot even reach down and touch your feet because your back hurts so bad."

It turned out that Ralph had suffered a work injury that had forced him onto disability. I explained that God could heal him in the same way that He had just healed his wife, but he declined saying, "Oh no, that's OK; I'll be all right." His wife immediately chimed in with, "Come on, Ralph, they prayed for me, and I am totally healed."

He reluctantly agreed to let us pray for him and began to take the large, unlit cigar out of his mouth. I explained to him that he did not need to remove the cigar that God already knew that he smoked cigars and that he had highlighted him knowing those details. I wanted Ralph to know that God was interested in his heart, not his cigar.

I asked if I could lay my hand on his back, which he agreed to, and then I prayed a simple prayer, "Lord, let Your presence come on his back. Bring Your Kingdom. I speak alignment in Jesus' name." I asked if he felt anything going on, to which he responded that he felt heat in his lower back where I had placed my hand.

I followed up by asking him to do something that he could not do, like touching his toes. At first he was hesitant, but through the encouragement of his wife and the rest of the team, he decided to make an attempt. As he hesitantly began to bend over to appease us, he realized that he had no more pain, but complete flexibility. He began to touch the ground over and over, bending with ease. He was totally healed. And, with cigar in mouth,

Ralph also prayed to invite Jesus into his life. That is the power of demonstration.

We Need to Talk

On another occasion, one day after church, I was with a small group of people having lunch at a local restaurant. One of the ladies who had joined us was visiting from out of state. I soon learned that she had advanced breast cancer and was not expected to live more than a few months. At the conclusion of lunch, I felt compelled to pray for her, so, right there in the middle of the restaurant, we all laid our hands on her and began to pray.

Suddenly, she began to cry out in agonizing wails. It turned out that she was being spiritually and emotionally tormented with demonic affliction. We quickly gathered around in order to protect her dignity, and in the next few minutes, quietly cast out the tormenting spirit that had been afflicting her. Suddenly, she broke into laughter through her tears that told everyone that she was free.

Meanwhile, the servers and manager had been keeping a keen eye on what was going on at our table over the previous 15 minutes. It just happened that one of our students from the Bethel School of Supernatural Ministry was working as a hostess at the restaurant that day. I periodically would go over to her, giving her the "play by play," which she passed on to the servers and manager.

After we left, the manager called our student, the hostess, into the back room for a "talk." He explained to her that he had never been to church and was not a Christian, but that he felt compelled to tell this student everything that he had ever done wrong in his life! He wanted to confess his sins after seeing the demonstration of the Spirit's power. Nobody preached a "repentance" message in the restaurant, and the student did not suggest that the manager repent of anything. No, when he saw the goodness of God revealed in a woman who was visibly set free, he also had a hunger to be set free.

The Bible tells us that it is the "kindness of God that leads us to repentance." Words of knowledge and the demonstration of the Spirit help us to communicate His kindness for "the common good." Words of knowledge let people know that God cares about their needs, no matter how seemingly insignificant or overwhelming their needs may be. They also communicate how God knows them in minute detail, which for many, proves that God exists and is interested in their lives.

It Is Easy to Hear From God

For many Christians, the idea of hearing from God is very foreign. Christians have no problem petitioning God, expecting Him to hear them. What they have difficulty with is believing that they hear from Him. Unfortunately, for many Christians, hearing from God has been reduced to getting an insight from the Bible. For some, the thought of God directly speaking to us individually is scary because of all of the "kooks" who have claimed to hear from God, but had obviously heard from another source.

Hearing from God personally *is* scriptural. For example, Moses had a conversation with God at the burning bush in which God gave him specific instructions to deliver the Israelites out of bondage in Egypt. (See Exodus 3.) Gideon gained confidence to take on the Midianites when the Angel of the Lord called out his true identity and gave him the confirmation through a "fleece" to accomplish his destiny. (See Judges 6:11-40.) Paul heard Jesus' voice on the road to Damascus, as mentioned earlier, and Peter had Jesus instruct him regarding the "clean and unclean" animals in Acts chapter 10.

In John 16:13, Jesus promised that:

> ...When He, the Spirit of truth, comes, He will guide you into all truth. He will not speak on His own; He will speak only what He hears, and He will tell you what is yet to come. He will bring glory to Me by taking from what is Mine and making it known to you.

The Holy Spirit has been given to us to communicate the plans and desires of the Father. The Holy Spirit does this through visions, dreams, prophetic words, words of wisdom, and words of knowledge (see 1 Cor. 12).

It is easy to hear from God. Take Samuel in the temple. He heard from God even though he did not know it was God. Three times he went to Eli, the High Priest, thinking it was he who had called. In 2 Samuel 3:7, we are told that "the word of the Lord had not yet been revealed to him." Finally, Eli instructed Samuel how to respond to the voice of the Lord, and when God spoke to him the next time, Samuel was able to discern God's voice.

"JUST MAKE ONE UP"

I believe God is speaking to all of us more than we are discerning. I often travel to various churches, equipping and activating the people to live naturally supernaturally. I was at a particular church over a weekend. During the Sunday morning service, I called the leadership team up front to give words of knowledge for healing. We went through many words of knowledge, with several people getting healed as the word was spoken.

We finally came to one of the key leaders of the church, and I asked him to give a word of knowledge. "I don't have one," he responded.

"Sure you do," I encouraged.

"No, I really don't have one."

"Then make one up," I implored.

The congregation gasped, and the leader looked at me in disbelief, and asked, "You're joking, right?"

"No, I'm serious; make one up," I pressed. The point I was trying to make was that hearing from God is a lot simpler than many of us imagine.

With a look of obvious consternation on his face, the leader grabbed the first word that came to his mind and blurted out, "Okay, someone here has lower stomach pain, and you feel very nauseated." Immediately, five people raised their hand, and all of them were completely healed on the spot. The church erupted in praise as all five of them confirmed their healing in public testimony.

The notion that "our thoughts are not His thoughts" is an Old Testament statement about a rebellious Israel whom the prophet Isaiah was imploring to repent (Isa. 55:8). To the obedient, to the Christian, the statement reads more like, "Our thoughts are His thoughts." The Bible is clear: It is the unbeliever who has the depraved mind (see Rom. 1:28), and that mind is hostile toward God (see Rom. 8:7). The believer, the Christian, on the other hand, is commanded to be transformed by the renewing of his/her mind (see Rom. 12:2).

Moreover, the apostle Paul tells us in First Corinthians 2:16 that we in fact "have the mind of Christ."

"How Do You Do It?"

Twice a year, we have "Pastors'/Leaders' Advances," a three-day event at which we have our second-year students, having been trained in hearing the voice of the Lord, prophesy over these leaders. Two students per team, along with a junior high school student from our Christian school, will then spend approximately ten minutes per person over a two-hour session.

On one occasion, two of our Supernatural Ministry students were paired up with a 12-year-old boy. As leaders were placed in front of them, the two older students would look at each other, asking whether or not they had a "word." Each time, they would both respond that they did not have something right away, then would defer to the junior high student who always responded with lengthy, encouraging "words."

After the two-hour session was over, the two School of Supernatural Ministry students were astonished at the competency level of the 12-year-old. When they asked how long he had been prophesying, thinking he was surely quite experienced, he responded that this was his first time. Shocked, the Supernatural Ministry students began to inquire how he got so many words—words that turned out to be very detailed and encouraging to the leaders they had been prophesying to.

His response was simple, "My teacher told me that I was going to prophesy today, so I figured since I was doing God's work, whatever thought came into my head was from God. So, when you asked if I had anything, I just said whatever first came to my mind." The School of Supernatural Ministry students instantly received a life-changing revelation regarding the simplicity of hearing God's voice.

Confidence in accessing and being activated in "words of knowledge" comes from 1) learning to tap into this "new" mind, the mind of Christ; 2) then like Samuel, learning to discern that what you are hearing is actually from God; and 3) taking a risk to see if what you heard helps "for the common good."

HE-BREWS COFFEE?

In preparation for a Treasure Hunt in Santa Rosa, California, Joaquín, one of our School of Supernatural Ministry students thought he heard "He-brews Coffee," which is the name of the coffee shop located in our church building. He immediately discarded that thought as flippant and inconsequential because it was so unlikely that the clue would have any significance some 250 miles away from Redding.

Throughout the preparation time (three minutes), I constantly reminded the group to go after "out of the box," seemingly senseless words of knowledge. "If you have a thought," I told them, "write it down, even if it seems impossible." The thought "He-brews Coffee" kept coming to this student's mind, but each time he dismissed it as his own, unrelated thought.

As he was going out with his Treasure Hunting team, he once again heard "He-brews Coffee" in his mind. This time, however, to appease his conscience, he decided to write it in very small letters at the very bottom of the page, well below the other clues he had heard and written down.

During their Treasure Hunt, their Map had directed them to a local park. While there, the student noticed a man sitting on a bench. With no apparent clues, the student was just building some rapport with the man in hopes of a door opening up to demonstrate the "Good News" to him in some way.

As they spoke, the conversation turned to spiritual inquiries. The man shared that he was not a Christian, but that if he were, the only church he would ever consider attending, would be a church in Redding, California: Bethel Church. He explained that his reason for wanting to go to that particular church was that they had a little coffee shop inside called "He-brews," with some of the best coffee he had ever tasted!

At once, the student pulled out the Treasure Map to show the man that this was a divine appointment. The man was amazed at the clue, and afterwards, was receptive to the "Good News" the student began to share. The student left the encounter with convincing proof that "His thoughts are our thoughts."

In conducting first-time Treasure Hunts, I always limit the time to get "words of knowledge" to three minutes. The first reason is that most of the people do not have confidence that they will hear from God even if they were to wait for three hours. I want them to have a practical experience of how easy it is to hear from God. And second, I do not want to give them too much time to change their minds as they do hear from God.

We always end the Treasure Hunt by meeting together as a large group so that all of the teams have a chance to share the testimonies of the Treasure they found. I am always thrilled when hearing the testimonies of those who did not believe their Map could have led to any Treasure whatsoever, and how they had found every clue on their Map, which led to over-the-top, extreme supernatural divine appointments in which people were saved, healed, and delivered.

THE TREASURE HUNT TEST

I will never forget one occasion on which I took a pastor out who was skeptical of the Treasure Hunt concept. As one of his clues, he jokingly wrote down "Eiffel Tower," knowing that we had no plans to travel to France, and therefore could prove that the Treasure Hunt was just "luck" if anything.

As we deciphered the other clues on the other team members' Maps, we were led to the local mall. In the mall, our clues directed us to an earring shop. As we walked into the store, not knowing what we would find, we suddenly noticed, hidden in the back corner, an "Eiffel Tower" earring stand!

The pastor was dumbfounded. "This is amazing," he repeated several times. We then found several other clues in the store that led us to be able to prophesy over the young woman at the counter and pray over the phone for her mother who was home on disability with an injured back; we had clues exactly describing her condition. The woman ended up getting healed over the phone, and we were able to pray with the young woman at the counter (her daughter) as well.

There have been so many, like this pastor, who have the concept that getting "words of knowledge" is only for the specifically gifted, and that this gift is only given on rare, "special" occasions. Over the past several years, I have witnessed how normal, ordinary Christians like Ananias have learned how to hear from God in the natural course of everyday life, as they have taken risks to become Ultimate Treasure Hunters.

Certainly, there are times when we think we have heard from God, only to find that we have somehow missed it. I would be the last person to say that I hear from God with 100 percent accuracy. Many times, I have finished a Treasure Hunt without finding all of the clues on my Map. I am still learning how to hear better. Nevertheless, I am always elated when I do hear clues that become keys to discovering the hidden treasures lying in unsuspected places that I have been directed to.

CHAPTER 4

Creating the Treasure Map

I N THE PREVIOUS CHAPTER, we discussed utilizing "words of knowledge" to give us the clues needed for the Treasure Hunt. In this chapter, we will get into some of the specific details of how the Treasure Map is created. In order to ensure the most successful Treasure Hunt, it is important that the Treasure Map is compiled in the format I will outline below. (Also, see Appendix A.)

Over the past few years, I have noticed five basic categories of clues that help uncover buried Treasure. Importantly, the specific detailed clues in all five of these categories are ascertained through words of knowledge. The categories of clues are:

- A location.

- A person's name.

- A person's appearance.

- A person's ailment—something he/she might need prayer for.

- The unusual.

While a Treasure Hunt can be launched from just a single category, I have found that having a lot of categories will help in opening the Treasure once it is found. For example, if someone has "dental office" on her list, it is more difficult to convince the person in the lobby that he is the sought-after Treasure, than if she had other specific clues like his name, what he was wearing, an ailment, or something unusual like "He-brews Coffee."

Obviously, if you have a person's name, then ask a random person if his name is "Ralph," his curiosity will most likely be peaked enough to allow you to at least let him know that God knows him specifically and obviously cares about him. That kind of divine appointment is often a "seed-planting" event, of which we will not know the effect until we arrive in Heaven.

I certainly appreciate the times when we get to encounter Treasures that we are preparing for someone else to open, but what really excites me is to find the Treasure, open it up, and bring it to the King, so that all of Heaven can rejoice. I love to bring people into the Kingdom of God so that they can experience all of the blessings I have found.

The more specific and extensive we are in presenting the clues, the more open people tend to be toward us, the Treasure Hunters. It is astonishing to watch the transformation in someone's countenance as you go down the list on your Treasure Map describing the details of her life that only God could have told you about. I have had some of the coldest people turn into best friends after seeing their clues on the Treasure Map.

Now of course, there are always those who will not respond even with two pages of clues specifically highlighting them. I will never forget the time I was doing a Treasure Hunt in a large department store. We saw a guy there who fulfilled at least ten clues on our Treasure Map. We approached him and showed him the Treasure Map in a very casual, non-threatening way, but as soon as the man finished looking at all of the clues, he literally ran away.

How sad that this man missed his opportunity. At the same time, I do not have insight into all of the strategic purposes of God. Who knows, maybe this man went home and thought about the divine encounter all day, then told his wife that he was now convinced that God is real. Whatever the case, we did our job in convincing fashion. The Holy Spirit is He who brings conviction and brings them into the Kingdom. Our job is to find the Treasure; His job is to salvage it.

Getting back to the point, when people see their clues written down, it is very difficult for them to deny that something "abnormal" is taking place. That is why using the Treasure Map is so important. Although telling someone that you received a clue about him as you were praying may get you entrance into his life if the word of knowledge is not visibly discernible, having it in writing is far more convincing.

For example, if you heard "red shirt," "blue socks," "sandals," and "cane" in your preparation for the Treasure Hunt, the person you are attempting to convince of the divine appointment will not as readily believe you because you could have "made up" the clues as you saw him from a distance. If they are written down, however, and in different categories on your Treasure Map, along with other non-related clues, the person will more than likely believe you. And more than that, he will most likely be shocked as though he had just been set up by *Candid Camera*.

LOCATION, LOCATION, LOCATION!

Having a location on your Treasure Map is helpful, but it is not mandatory. If you do not sense a "word" regarding the specific place you are to look for the Treasure, then just "make one up;" in other words, just start wherever seems good. Having a location simply helps to create more confidence in going and confidence upon arriving to find several other obscure clues that could only have been found at the location on your Treasure Map.

Sometimes the location clues are found in the "unusual" category and must be creatively interpreted to discover the location in which you will find the Treasure. I was on a Treasure Hunt one time on which one of our team members had "lollipop" and "windmill." We had found several other clues at the locations we had been directed to by the "location" category of our Treasure Map, but these other two clues were eluding us.

I suggested that we ask for creative insight into deciphering the clues we had been given. "Where could we find a 'windmill'?" I quizzed. One of the team members suggested that the local miniature golf course might have a "windmill" on one of the holes, and that maybe we were to meet someone on the course. So we hopped in the car and drove over to the miniature golf course that had just opened about a half an hour before. Immediately, we noticed a "windmill" on one of the holes; however, nobody had ventured out onto the course.

We wandered around the game section of the amusement park for a few minutes, checking out the dozen or so people who were there to see if we could find anyone sucking on a "lollipop." No lollipops. We were getting ready to head back to the church to share the other amazing testimonies of treasures we had found, when I noticed that in the glass case where they display all of the little prizes redeemed by coupons won at the various games was a large compartment filled with hundreds of lollipops.

I went over to the display case housing the lollipops and waited. Soon the others noticed the clue I had found and joined me. Not long after, a teenage girl came over to help us. We explained that we were on a Treasure Hunt, and that we had "lollipop" on our list of locations that we were searching out.

At that, the teenage girl responded, "That is the best line I've ever heard from someone trying to get a lollipop. Here you can all have a free lollipop."

"No, no," I countered, "we do not want a lollipop. We are supposed to meet someone whom God wants to encourage in some way."

She shot back, "No, really, that is the best line I have ever heard. You all get a free lollipop."

Once again I explained about the Treasure Hunt and that we really did not want a lollipop. Then it dawned on me that she might be the Treasure that we were supposed to find at this location.

I said to her, "Maybe you are the one we are supposed to speak to today? Maybe you are the Treasure that we are looking for?" At once, her eyes filled with tears as she told us that just that morning she had asked for a sign. She had asked God to show her what she was supposed to do about her alcoholic mother who seemed to be "bottoming out" and taking the rest of the kids with her.

She explained that she was the oldest in a "single mom" family and was left with the responsibility of taking care of her alcoholic mother as well as her younger siblings. Just that morning, she had come to the end of her strength, and while she had not gone to church but a few times, she cried out to God for help.

We began to prophesy destiny over her life, that God had a good plan for her and her mother. We further expressed God the Father's love for her, in that He would send us to answer her prayer. The tears began to flow, as she became more and more cognizant of the divine encounter at the "lollipops."

I could see that the manager was growing increasingly nervous as he was watching our interaction from across the room. As he started to make his way toward us, the young girl motioned and yelled out over her now hoarse-sounding voice that everything was fine and that she was not being harassed in any way. Over the next few minutes, we continued to encourage her and gave her some wisdom in dealing with her mother. Afterward, she told us that we truly were an answer to her prayer and felt like she had the strength and insight to make some positive changes.

Sometimes the clues for the location in which we are to go Treasure Hunting are obvious. Many times they are not. And then, there is the timing in which you arrive at a specific location that is crucial to finding hidden Treasure. Often, I will go to several sites that I have clues for on the Treasure Map and not find any Treasure there. At the fourth site, I find the Treasure, and realize that if I had not gone to the other sites first, I would have missed the divine appointment, who also had just arrived a few minutes before.

A Person's Name

Having a person's name may be the clue with the greatest impact on your Treasure Map. While other clues may grab the attention of the person you are Treasure Hunting for, having her name as a clue on your Treasure Map makes it undeniably personal for her. For example, when we met "Ralph" at Home Depot, having his name opened the door for a divine appointment. When he heard me call out his name, he went from a skeptical bystander to being healed and having an extreme encounter with God.

I wonder if Saul in Acts 9 would have had the same immediate reaction if Jesus had only yelled down from Heaven, "Why are you persecuting Me?" instead of calling out his name two times to get his attention. There was no doubt; Jesus was talking to him and no one else. Saul did not respond, "Who me?" but, rather, he said, "Who are you?" Because he was called by name, Saul was reeled into a divine encounter.

There is just something about someone knowing your name that makes you feel special. Moreover, when people find out their name was singled out by God to someone whom they had never met, they are often overwhelmed by the thought that God actually does know them specifically by name. It is as though they hear the words of Isaiah 43:1, "I have summoned you by name; you are Mine." Frequently, that personal call causes people to open up and respond to the invitation to receive God's blessings for their lives.

Zacchaeus' interest was certainly peaked enough in Luke 19 that he climbed up a sycamore-fig tree to see Jesus and try to find out who He was. It is implied in the text, that Jesus also did not know Zacchaeus other than by word of knowledge. We are told that when Jesus reached the spot where Zacchaeus was "hanging" out, he looked up and said to him, "Zacchaeus, come down immediately. I must stay at your house today." And without hesitation, Zacchaeus came down and "welcomed Him gladly." (See Luke 19:1-6.) This encounter is an excellent illustration of the effectiveness of having a name on your Treasure Map.

I was doing a Treasure Hunt in Indiana, and our team was directed to a Wal-Mart. We had several divine appointments as we followed our Treasure Map around the store looking for the various clues. On the way out, one of the women on our team started running toward one of the employed greeters. Still from a distance, she began to yell out "Stu! Stu!" as if he were an old friend. When she got to him, she greeted him with an excited smile and a familiar hug. Then, with a concerned look on her face, she began to ask how he was doing.

As we followed, thinking the woman had run into a long-time acquaintance, we soon realized that "Stu" was a total stranger because of the stunned look on his face. As it turned out, she had the name "Stu" on her Treasure Map and had been looking for him during the entire Treasure Hunt. When she saw his name badge from afar, she knew he was the Treasure she had been looking for.

As it turned out, Stu had several other clues such as "glasses," a "heart condition," and a wife who was home afflicted with "cancer." It was not long before he was so overwhelmed by the fact that we had his name written down on our Treasure Map that he let us pray for him right there in the doorway to the store. By the end of the ten-minute divine encounter, we all were like long-time friends with Stu, to the point he gave us his phone number and address, so that we could follow up with prayer for his wife's healing.

A PERSON'S APPEARANCE

In addition to having a specific location and a name, having the details of a person's appearance can be just as convincing proof that God has directed you to the Treasure. Whether the clue contains the color of their hair, their gender, age, or the clothes they are wearing, knowing their appearance often makes it much easier to get them to believe that God has sent you to help them.

Obviously, there could be hundreds of people at a local Target store to which you were led from your Treasure Map. There could be dozens of Johns. But how many "Johns" could there be with dyed hair, a blue and white shirt, black converse sneakers, black shorts, and a tattoo on his right leg. Those details significantly narrow down the "Johns" walking around the store.

I remember on one occasion walking into a supermarket and seeing a woman who fit the description on my Treasure Map. I approached her saying, "Excuse me, but we are on a Treasure Hunt, and I think you are on our Map."

"No, I'm not," she responded.

I followed up by reading off the list of details that I had on my Map. She took the Map from me and began to study it. After a few minutes, she looked up with resignation and agreed that she was indeed on our Map.

She then began to cry because there was another clue on the Map that we could have never known about, but as she was scanning the clues that we had pointed out about her appearance, she noticed that "tumor" had been listed as one of the clues under the "ailment" category and began to divulge that she had just been diagnosed as having a cancerous tumor on her cervix.

When we offered to pray for her, she gladly accepted, saying she had never known that God cared about her since she had always been an atheist. We prayed for her, and she felt a fire in the cervical area, and a fire in her heart when she asked Jesus to be her Savior. Had it not been for the detailed list of "personal appearance" clues that were written down for this woman to read, we would never have been granted access into the secrets of her life and would not have had the opportunity to pray for her deepest need.

A PERSON'S AILMENTS: WHAT THEY MIGHT NEED PRAYER FOR

Sometimes on a Treasure Hunt, the only solid clue I have is something like "knee brace" or "hurt knee." With that one clue, however, I will search in the locations that I am directed to on the Map, or just start hunting wherever I think is best at the time. Normally, it is not long until I find someone limping or wearing a knee brace. At that, I can confidently approach him or her with the good news that he or she is the Treasure God wants to heal in order to demonstrate His kindness.

There have been countless testimonies of finding Treasures by focusing on the "ailment" clue, especially when the ailment is obvious and written on your Map. On one occasion, one of the teams had "limp." They had been directed to a mall and had been looking for various clues on their Treasure Map, when they noticed a teenaged boy limping off an escalator.

Cherise, one of our interns in the School of Supernatural Ministry, approached the young teenager and explained the Treasure Hunt, indicating that God had highlighted him. She noticed that the teenager had a brace on his foot and then showed him the Treasure Map on which she had written, "limp." She began to point out that God wanted to heal his ankle that had just been severely sprained during the previous soccer game and asked if he would be willing to let her pray for him.

Stunned by seeing his ailment on Cherise's Treasure Map, he agreed to let her pray. She simply commanded all the pain to leave in the name of Jesus, then instructed him to test it out. He began to jump up and down on the injured foot and proclaimed that he had no pain whatsoever.

Wanting the teenage boy to be sure it was OK, she asked him to do something else that he could not have previously done before she prayed for him. He took off sprinting wildly across the courtyard in the mall and came back totally healed. The teenager's friends stood there amazed at what they had just witnessed.

It was then that two older teenagers, who knew the teen who was healed, came over to mock what was happening. The healed teen began to defend the authenticity of what had just happened, that God had just healed him, but the older teenagers just continued their abusive dialogue.

Cherise jumped in the middle of the verbal scuffle, and pointing to the most verbal of the mocking teenagers, asked "Does your leg hurt also?" Taken aback with this insight, he sheepishly confessed that it did, pointing to his thigh.

"God wants to heal you. Can I pray for you?" Cherise pursued.

"Well, I guess, if you want to," replied the now compliant, but still, a guarded teenager.

"Oh, I want to," Cherise shot back.

And at that, she began to command the pain to leave, and without a thought, slapped his leg as hard as she could (not a technique we promote at the school). The teenager began to jump up and down, spinning and squatting, while simultaneously yelling at Cherise, "What the f... did you do? What the h..., oh my God!" He then began to proclaim that he had been totally healed and boldly testified of the miracle to everyone around. No more mocking and no more cussing.

Cherise began to share the gospel with everyone who had now gathered around, and each one of them was enthusiastically receptive. As the team began to walk away, another of the teenage boys stopped her and asked if she could pray for his knee really quickly as the group of teenagers needed to go by then. "Of course I can. The Lord heals you," and without her even laying her hands on him, all of the pain left, and he ran off to join his friends who had already begun to make their way out of the mall, totally healed!

All of this happened because Cherise wrote down "limp." That word of knowledge not only opened the door for her to pray for three teenagers and witness to a small crowd but also gave her the confidence to take the risks needed to break through in the situation. Having these clues written down elevated everyone's faith and paved the way for another divine encounter in the quest for the Ultimate Treasure.

The Unusual

By now, you are probably thinking to yourself, "Unusual. *All* of this stuff is unusual." I would like to suggest that the Treasure Hunt is unusual until you do it enough so that it becomes usual. We will talk about living "naturally" supernatural in a later chapter, which I hope will help clarify how we can live a "normal" supernatural lifestyle in which the "unusual" becomes usual.

By "unusual," I am speaking of clues that you receive that do not fit into any of the above categories. They may turn out to be a location or part of a person's appearance, but initially you cannot discern any connection. So, you put it in the "unusual" category while you look for clarification.

My daughter, who was 12 at the time, was on a Treasure Hunt with me during a "Firestorm" weekend (see Appendix B). Under the "unusual" category she had "lime-green door," "lamp posts," and "thermometers." Now the "lamp posts" could have been placed under the category of "location," but as it turned out later, there were no street-lights in the part of the city we were in, let alone "lamp posts." This turned out to be a very unusual clue indeed.

As we walked around the neighborhood near the church where we were having the conference, we noticed a brightly glossed, multi-colored house in the distance. It looked like something out of "Toon Town" at Disneyland. This house was amazing! Every part of the house was painted a different vibrant color—blues, reds, yellows, and purples, all over a white base that caused each color to be further pronounced.

As we got closer, we noticed that there was no "green" on the house, not to mention the "lime green" we were looking for. When we came to the house, we were astonished to see several "lamp posts" lining the walkway up toward the front door that was somewhere tucked around the corner from where we were standing. We looked around and realized these were the only "lamp posts" visible. What an amazing clue, given the surroundings.

As we stood there, I flippantly commented, "Wouldn't it be funny if the front door was lime green?" We ventured up the walkway to investigate the "lime-green door" clue, when we noticed that on outer walls between the detached garage and the main house were five huge, round weather "thermometers." Why anyone would ever need five, especially in the same location, is beyond me, but each to his own. It made Alexa's "unusual" clue even that much more unusual.

By now, all of the blood in us was pumping in anticipation for the discovery of the color of the front door, which was still hidden around the corner. We looked around again at parts of the house that revealed more creative color schemes, but still, no green anywhere. "If this house has a 'lime-green door' that in itself will be a miracle," I quipped.

As we rounded the corner, we all were dumbfounded. The front door was, in fact, "lime green." We knocked on the door vigorously, knowing that our divine appointment was waiting inside, but apparently, nobody was home. Our hearts began to sink in disappointment, knowing that these "unusual," miraculous clues might be wasted because of wrong timing.

The house was multi-level and had several entrances, and thinking someone was in another part of the house where they could not hear the front doorbell, we checked every alternative without any response. It seemed that we had struck out, that there was no Treasure to be found, even though our Treasure Map had led us to this unusual house. So we prayed that God would grant supernatural encounters to those who lived there, and that He would reveal His love to them in undeniable ways.

Just as we were leaving, I noticed that the grounds were covered in various trees and flower gardens. Hope for a divine appointment resurged in the team, and we set about looking for someone in the sprawling gardens located on the property. Just when we were about to give up the search, I noticed a man bent over down in an obscure part of one of the gardens. Yes! We had found our Treasure!

We climbed down to where he was gardening and explained about how we had come upon his house through the clues on our Treasure Map. He was shocked as he studied the Treasure Map, but informed us that he was not the owner of the house, that he was a local contractor who just enjoyed coming over to work in the garden for "therapeutic" purposes.

He kept quizzing us as to how we "really" found the house and kept asking us what we really wanted, insinuating that we were running some kind of highly sophisticated scam. We assured him that we did not want anything from him, but that we wanted to bless him in some way. We let him know that we were not even from the state, and never could have known about this house, with the "unusual" clues we had written down, unless God had given us the information.

We began to share with him how God reveals His goodness in these types of encounters by letting the people we meet know that He has specifically highlighted them. He confessed that he was not a Christian, but that he was very intrigued with the clues we had and the message we were conveying.

The man accepted our prayers and the prophetic words we spoke to him regarding the plan that God had for his life. When we returned to give testimonies, another group shared about how they were led to the same house through completely different clues. The man in the garden was so overwhelmed by the unusual circumstances of two Treasure Hunting teams finding him that he allowed the team to lead him in a prayer to accept Christ into his heart!

USING THE TREASURE MAP

By now, you can probably see the importance of writing the clues down on the Treasure Map. Just as important is the way you use the Treasure Map in your search for hidden Treasure. I always make a point to fold the Map in half so that it is obscure during the hunt, but visible enough for me to continually scan it for clues that may come my way.

I'm sure there have been many clues that were right there in front of me, but because I was not looking at my Map enough, I passed by without a clue (excuse the pun). That is why, when Treasure Hunting on a team, you look at each other's Maps, so that the clues have a better chance of being discovered. I have found so many clues for hidden Treasure on other people's Maps just because I happened to glance at one of the clues at the right time.

It is also important to note that you may only have one of the clues that, combined with several others, from different teammates, may lead you to a Treasure that you would have never been able to discover on your own. We will get into some of the details of group Treasure Hunting in the next chapter.

CHAPTER 5

Getting Started on the Treasure Hunt

᭒᭑᭢᭑᭒

IMAGINE A TREASURE HUNTING EXPEDITION in which the team invested thousands of dollars and countless hours over many years doing research in hopes of finding the ultimate treasure. They met every week to discuss the specific location of this hidden treasure, and each week, they went over various strategies for uncovering the treasure once they found it. They counted the cost and determined that the treasure was worth going after. Finally, they even put ads in the paper, inviting other potential Treasure Hunters because they realized that the job was too big for them alone. They continued to meet together each week.

What is wrong with this picture? The answer is easy: They never went! Unfortunately, this is a picture of too many churches and too many Christians. Often, as church leaders, we have thoroughly equipped the church with every resource needed to become the Ultimate Treasure Hunter, yet week after week, the church returns for more "strategic" meetings, while the hidden Treasures throughout their communities remain lost. We act as though we were expecting the lost Treasure to find its way into our churches even though they are blind and lost and, therefore, cannot find their way. We must find them, and that requires "going."

JUST DO IT!

I once heard a prominent church leader sadly quip, "Christians have been taught way beyond their obedience." This is a regrettable but true statement as it relates to the evangelistic responsibility of every Christian and every church. The message of the Bible is clear: We are to "**go and make disciples of all nations...teaching them to obey everything** I have commanded you" (Matt. 28:19-20).

James sums up this point well in his Epistle when he instructs, "Do not merely listen to the Word, and so deceive yourselves. Do what it says" (James 1:22). Only so much talk should be tolerated before someone jumps up and shouts, "Let's go do it." Of course this could be applied to any of the themes of teaching throughout the Scriptures.

I have heard many Christians over the years demand pastors to give them "the meat of the Word." What they mean, however, is that they want an insightful Bible study that will give them more knowledge. Obviously, we must train Christians in the truths of Scripture, which requires a foundation of information. But information (knowledge) is not the "meat" of the Word.

Jesus was clear on this point. He said, "*My food [meat]... is to do the will of Him who sent me and to finish His work*" (John 4:34). He goes on to exhort the disciples to *"open their eyes and look at the fields! They are ripe for harvest."* I want to suggest that doing God's will, eating the meat of the Word, is not doing a Bible study or listening to a Bible study, but going and doing what it says, especially as it relates to working in the ripe harvest fields, which is the aim of the Treasure Hunt.

Like Ananias in our study of Acts chapter 9, the hardest part of the Adventure is the *going*. He did not question whether or not God had spoken to him. He knew God's voice, and knew that what He had spoken was true. His concern and initial hesitation were in the command to "Go!" He was afraid.

Keep in mind, Ananias was probably not a natural-born risk taker. In reality, he was probably a timid, introverted guy by nature. I can almost hear him thinking, "Hey, instead of *going*, why don't I start a prayer meeting at the church to specifically pray for this guy Saul? After all, prayer is powerful and effective, and by the way, a lot safer!" Thankfully, against all fear and intimidation, Ananias went, fulfilling Jesus' command to "Go!" And of course, when we do "go," amazingly, we find Treasures beyond our wildest expectations.

I recently heard a report of a man who discovered an extremely valuable 4.21-carat, crystal-shaped diamond at the Crater of Diamonds State Park in Arkansas. Interestingly, this man had no training in diamond excavation and was not an expert in gemology. As a State Trooper he was just looking for a creative adventure to enjoy with his family.

As it turns out, there have been over 25,000 diamonds unearthed in this park since 1972, which amounts to about two discoveries per day by visitors. It only costs $6.00 to enter the park, yet few seem to take advantage of the opportunity to Treasure Hunt. Those who do "go," however, have a chance at uncovering a diamond like the "Uncle Sam," a 40.23-carat, which is the largest diamond ever found at the park and in the United States.

I want to suggest that Treasure Hunting provides an amazing opportunity to discover hidden gems. There are people just waiting for you to pay the price to come and find them. You do not have to be an expert Treasure Hunter. You do not have to be an astute theologian. But you do have to take some risk and go!

DETERMINING TO TAKE RISK

I was leading an outreach one day in a neighborhood near our church. We had split up into two teams, going to various locations at which we knew would be divine appointments. At the end of the allotted time, we were to rendezvous at a certain location, and then head back to the church together.

After waiting for ten minutes, we understood that the other team had been caught up in a lengthy, divine appointment. I decided to send my other two teammates off to find them and report back the details of their delay, while I would stay at the designated location in case they came back before my team could find them.

As I was standing on the curb, waiting for the teams to arrive, I noticed a young man walking toward me on the sidewalk. As he approached from about 50 yards away, a thought popped into my mind, "Roger." *Is that a word of knowledge?* I asked. All that I heard in response was,

"Roger." By this time, the young man was about 20 yards away and quickly approaching. One more time I inquired, *God, please let me know if this is a word of knowledge, and that You want me to minister to this young man.* Once again, I heard "Roger."

The young man was now within ten yards, so I decided to take a risk and test out this word of knowledge I had received. So, as he began to pass me on the sidewalk, I said with as much confidence as I could muster, "Excuse me, but is your name Roger?" I asked fully expecting that to be his name which would lead to an incredible divine appointment.

But, with a look of disdain, he jumped off the sidewalk, and said "Noooo!" as if I were trying to "pick up" on him. As he continued to walk down the street, I was filled with embarrassment, as it occurred to me how odd it was for a 45-year-old man to ask a 20-year-old if his name was "Roger."

Now, if his name had been Roger, I'm sure his response would have been different, but in this case, it just came off like I was some sort of predator. I thought about chasing him down to explain, but immediately realized that I would probably just make things worse. And then I thought, *At least I did not say that God had told me that his name was Roger; at least I did not defame Christianity. He just thought I was a kook.*

My next thought was, *Thanks a lot, God. I just made a fool out of myself because I took a risk with a word of knowledge I thought You had given me.* The response I heard shocked me, "Kevin, I gave you the name 'Roger.'"

"What? You purposely gave me the wrong name?" I shot back.

"Yes, I did, because I want to see if you will continue to take risk even if you do not get the right information." He went on to say that He was not interested in the success of the performance, but in the act of obedience, apart from the outcome.

I know this story is out of the box for many, and I would not suggest that God is in the habit of giving false words of knowledge to test our resolve. But for me, it was a unique and specific lesson about how God is more interested in the level of my risk-taking than the level of my success. I still miss, but not because God gives me the wrong word; that was a one-time occurrence; rather I miss because I am still learning to discern the voice of the Lord. What I have learned, however, is that every step of risk is rewarded equally, regardless of the results. God rewards faith not the performance.

MISTAKES ARE GOOD

I was doing a Firestorm conference at a large church, in which at one point, I released our second-year School of Supernatural Ministry students to give prophetic words to individuals who were seated in the audience. Most of the words were very accurate and encouraging, but a few missed the mark of accuracy as a few of the students took a risk to share what they thought they had heard from God.

The following week when I called to get some feedback from the weekend, the pastor shared that he had some concern that some of the content of a few of the prophetic words was not accurate. He was concerned that having some wrong words might negate the many right ones and, moreover, diminish the credibility of the team's efforts in general. The pastor, however, did acknowledge appreciation in how I had publicly acknowledged the "wrong" word at the time and subtly fixed it with a "right" word.

I offered that it was better to have some wrong words stand out to let the people know that it is all right to make mistakes, that you do not have to maintain 100 percent accuracy to prophesy according to the New Testament.

First of all, Jesus identified "false prophets" by the fruit of their character, not the accuracy of their words (Matt. 7:15-20). In other words, a false prophet can have a right word, which conversely implies that a true prophet can have a wrong word. Therefore, having a wrong word does not make someone a false prophet.

Second, the apostle Paul instructs in First Corinthians 14:29, "Two or three prophets should speak, and the others should weigh carefully what is said." If the prophetic was expected to be mistake-free, then there would have been no need to "weigh" or, as in some translations, "judge" the words that were spoken. Once again, God is more interested in the level of risk we take with a pure heart to bless those around us, than our playing it safe with what we are absolutely sure of.

Because of a misunderstanding of the role of the Old Testament prophet, many have shied away from taking risk for fear of being stoned over a mistake. It is the same with witnessing. There is such fear in somehow failing in the encounters that God has set up for us that we tend to ignore the responsibility, rather than take a risk. But without risk, there is no reward. "Without faith, it is impossible to please God" (see Heb. 11:6).

PETER'S KEY TO BREAKTHROUGH: GETTING DRUNK

The apostle Peter is very typical of someone who was transformed from the ultra-intimidated to the fearlessly-bold. Remember, it was Peter who denied Christ three times when confronted by those who accused him of being one of His disciples (Matt.26:69-75). Fear robbed him of the impetus to walk in his God-given authority and fulfill his destiny.

After Jesus was crucified, we find the disciples, including Peter, hiding out, locked in the upper room for fear of the Jews (see John 20:19). In fact, once they discovered the empty tomb, it was not until Jesus appeared to them that they gained enough confidence to go out of doors. Even after being taught by Jesus for 40 days, they conducted church services behind closed doors (see Acts 1:13-14; 2:1), and not one occurrence is mentioned of a public witness of any kind. Although Peter and the rest of the disciples had all of the training required, they were still incapacitated while they waited for the impetus they needed to "go."

On the Day of Pentecost something changed. The promised Holy Spirit was poured out to the Church (see Acts 2:4), and along with this baptism, came a holy boldness that defied even the most intimidating threats. The Holy Spirit gave them the ability to be the witnesses they were called to be, just as Jesus had promised in Acts 1:8, when He said, "You will receive power when the Holy Spirit comes on you; and you will be My witnesses...." The key to

Peter's breakthrough in becoming a crazy, bold witness was in his being filled with the Holy Spirit—or, to put it in other terms, to be drunk!

You see, drunk people do crazy things. They will say the craziest things to anyone who will listen (or even if they won't listen). They will laugh out loud, often for no apparent reason and without any sensitivity to their surroundings whatsoever. They will dance, fall on the ground, sway as they walk, and completely sacrifice their personal dignity. Why? Because they are drunk, and drunk people do crazy things!

Drunk people are not concerned with what people think about them at the moment. They have lost all fear of man, not concerning themselves in the least with the aftermath of humiliation that is sure to follow their actions. They, therefore, express themselves freely. They will even attempt the dangerous, like driving a vehicle or jumping off cliffs into shallow water, crazy things that they would never even dream of doing if they were sober. Why? Because they are drunk, and drunk people do crazy things!

In Ephesians 5:18, the apostle Paul gives this instruction to Christians: "Do not get drunk on wine, which leads to debauchery. Instead, be filled with the Spirit."

This word "debauchery" means to be so influenced by the effects of alcohol that people lose all inhibition, so that they do things of negative and evil consequence that they would not do if they were sober. In other words, debauchery is doing crazy things that you are really ashamed of the next morning. Being filled with the Spirit, on the other hand, causes one to do crazy things, but the difference is that those things are things that you are proud of the next morning.

Interestingly, the phrase, "be filled," is not a one-time event. In the Greek, this is a present-tense verb, which has a continual sense associated with the action. So, more accurately, Paul is instructing the Church to "be continually filled with the Spirit"—to drink every day the "new wine" of the Spirit. Why? Because continually drunk people continually do crazy things.

Although the Day of Pentecost was the inauguration of the Holy Spirit to the Church, it was not to be the end of the infilling. The festival being celebrated that day was also called the "Feast of Firstfruits." It was a celebration of bringing in the first of the spring harvest, with the promise that God's provision would never end.

The intention God had for the Church was that the infilling of Acts 2:4 would never stop. That is why we are told in Acts 4:31, that "after they prayed, the place where they were meeting was shaken. And they were all *filled* with the Holy Spirit and spoke the word of God boldly." Note the connection between being filled with the Spirit and having boldness to witness. The best Treasure Hunters are drunk Treasure Hunters.

On the Day of Pentecost, when the Church was filled with the Holy Spirit, we are told that the crowd made fun of them and said, "They have had too much wine." Peter's response to this accusation is found in verse 15 of Acts chapter 2: "These men are not drunk as you suppose...."

Notice here that he does not deny the fact that they are drunk or, at least, acting drunk. He simply lets them know that the people who are filled with the Holy Spirit are not drunk in the way that they think that they are drunk.

The source of their drunkenness is not the wine of the world, rather the new wine of the Holy Spirit. He explains all of this in the context of the fulfilled prophetic promise of Joel: "In the last days, God says, I will pour out My Spirit on all people" (Acts 2:17).

On the Day of Pentecost, Peter got out of the box, crazy, as he found the courage to stand up to address the crowd of onlookers. This is the same Peter who denied the Lord three times! And now he has unabashed boldness to preach the Gospel to the same angry crowd that had earlier crucified Jesus. The only thing that can explain this uninhibited behavior is the fact that he was drunk. Drunk people do crazy things! And I'm sure he was very proud of his actions the next morning, especially when he realized that 3,000 people had been saved as a result of his boldness under the influence of the Spirit!

As we mentioned in earlier chapters, Jesus has commanded us to do crazy things like heal the sick, raise the dead, cleanse lepers, and cast out demons—to preach the message of the Kingdom (see Matt. 10:7-8). He has commanded us to be His witnesses in the whole earth as His ambassadors (see 2 Cor. 5:20). He told Ananias, through a supernatural vision, to go to Saul's house on Straight Street and lay hands on him to receive his sight, which was a crazy proposal given the fact that Saul was arresting Christians and giving approval for the executions (see Acts 8:1).

I have found that most people have a hard time stepping out in risk in the Kingdom because they are too intimidated by what others might think, or the repercussions of such actions. I want to suggest, that like Peter on the Day of Pentecost, you try getting absolutely drunk on the Spirit of

God until you have no inhibitions left, and just see what kind of great "crazy" things God can do through your life in finding the Ultimate Treasure.

I used to have a hard time stepping out in risk, but interestingly, after learning to let the Holy Spirit influence my mind, I began to "live under the influence" (LUI). I began to do things that I would ordinarily never try like praying for someone to be healed in public, or prophesying crazy insights about people I had never met that unlocked the Treasure buried inside of them. And amazingly, because I started taking risk, because I started "going," people started getting healed, saved, and delivered.

I began to "drink and drive," and when I would get to my destination, I would find supernatural boldness to step out and take crazy amounts of risk to pray for the sick and engage people in supernatural divine encounters at super-markets, airports, or at family gatherings. But it is not like I have developed a constant level of boldness in my life experience. It is not like I wake up every day with confidence to do the impossible. No, I constantly have to fight the urge to be frightened, which is why I need to be filled with so much more of the Holy Spirit each and every day.

Moreover, the more I drink, the bolder I get. And the bolder I get, the more risk I take. And the more risk I take the more Treasure I find, and that reward makes the going worthwhile. Like Peter who forgot about his fear and stepped into his destiny, I, too, am more able to fulfill mine as I am more empowered by the Spirit. My hope is that every believer experiences the available empowerment to break through and become the Ultimate Treasure Hunter.

Do We Have to Go Treasure Hunting?

Now certainly, experiencing the constant infilling of the Holy Spirit boosts one's confidence to take extraordinary risk, but as a believer, you already have the Holy Spirit, and when you go, He will be with you to help you even if you do not "feel" Him.

During our church's annual Jesus Culture youth conference we release some 800 to 1,000 Treasure Hunters out into our community as part of our goal to activate the youth in the supernatural. We always get back amazing testimonies of people who had never before witnessed in public, yet were able to pray for the sick and injured, prophesy, and lead people to Christ utilizing the Treasure Hunt.

I will never forget the group of about 60 I once led to our local mall. After I had divided the group into teams of three or four and given them instructions to go find Treasure, I noticed that one of the teams was not paying attention and was looking very unhappy. I tried to ignore their attitude for a few minutes, but they soon started joking about the "stupidity" of the Treasure Hunt out loud.

I found out that their parents had dropped them off at the conference and told them that they had to attend everything. It was obvious that the two teenage brothers and sister did not want to be there. I told them that they did not have to do the Treasure Hunt, but they did have to carry their Treasure Maps and walk through the mall as though they were doing one.

Every once in a while, I would make a point to direct my team over to where they were so that I could check up on them. Each time, I would ask them how things were going and if they had found anything on their Treasure Map even though they were not doing the Treasure Hunt. I would also share the testimonies from our team and others that were happening all around them.

Each time, the two teenage brothers would respond in a mocking way that the only Treasures they had found were the pretty girls they had scoped out. I kept encouraging them to look at the Treasure Map, that God had put some clues on there to help them find a divine appointment. They would just laugh and make a comment about God helping them find a girlfriend before they had to go back to the conference.

We finally all met out in the parking lot at the designated time and began to share testimonies of the Treasure we had uncovered in the mall. Several teams had shared when I realized that the brothers and sister had not arrived on time. It was just then that they appeared across the parking lot jumping up and down and screaming at the top of their lungs, "We found one! We found one! She had everything on our Treasure Map! Even the butterfly-painted toenails."

When they made it back to the group, they were all smiles and were unable to contain themselves. They admitted that earlier they had no intentions of looking for Treasures, other than trying to pick up on girls, but after hearing the testimonies, they decided to look at their Maps before leaving the mall.

After looking their Maps over, they looked up, and the woman standing in front of them had every clue listed on all three Maps. They confessed to the woman that they had not believed in the Treasure Hunt and were just there because their parents had made them go, but now, there was no denying it: The Treasure Map worked; the woman was standing right there in front of them.

They then told us that the reason they were late was that they were praying for the woman to be healed of cancer. They went on and on about how God touched the woman who said she felt something happening, but could not confirm being healed. The teenagers were so filled with faith after that encounter, however, that it would be hard to imagine her not being healed.

There is Treasure waiting all around us. The price of admission is risk. We must go, whether the motivation and confidence comes through the infilling of the Holy Spirit or the sheer obedience to our heavenly Father's command. And when we go, there is always the possibility of finding the Ultimate Treasure!

CHAPTER 6

Techniques for a Successful Treasure Hunt

꙳꙳꙳

Now THAT WE ARE ALL FILLED AND MOTIVATED to go Treasure Hunting, I thought it would be a good idea to share some principles and techniques I have learned over the years to make your Treasure Hunt successful. "But wait a minute," you might protest, "I just read that God is not interested in success." No, what I said was that God is *more* interested in our level of faith to take risk than in our performance or success, and He rewards the former, not the latter. In other words, you get the same reward regardless of whether or not you find the Treasure. Nevertheless, God desires to be successful in every endeavor He pursues, including finding hidden Treasure.

Having success in the Treasure Hunt is not based upon having all of the right clues, or every clue for the Treasure you are trying to locate. There have been plenty of times in which I have found Treasure with just one or two seemingly insignificant clues. There have been other times in which I have found hidden Treasure with no clues whatsoever, just on my way to another Treasure location on my Map. Conversely, I have had several specific clues identifying a person as the Treasure, but was unable to recover them for some reason.

In this chapter, my goal is to outline some principles and techniques that will help you gain entrance into people's lives, so that you are able to bring the "good news" that can set them free and launch them into their designed destiny. I want to give you keys to developing trust with the people you meet so that you are more likely to be granted favor and influence in every Treasure Hunting encounter you have.

EVERYONE IS A SALESMAN

To begin, it is imperative to understand that every person is in sales. Simply put, sales is influence, and everyone at some level desires or is required to influence others in some way to accomplish various goals. Whether a young man attempting to woo the woman of his dreams to marry him, or a mother trying to convince little Johnny not to play in the street, we all engage in sales to move others toward a feeling, thought, action, or direction.

God is the ultimate salesman. He has been working toward influencing mankind since the Garden of Eden when He told Adam and Eve not to eat of the tree of the knowledge of good and evil. Of course, they would not "buy" God's instructions and came under the influence of the devil. But God immediately began selling the promise of salvation in Genesis 3:15. All throughout the Old Testament, God was pleading with His people to let Him influence them so that they would be blessed. Of course, over and over He was rejected even though He offered what they truly needed.

We might even say that God is the ultimate door-to-door salesman. In the Book of Revelation, Jesus proclaimed, "Here I am! I stand at the door and knock. If anyone hears My voice and opens the door, I will come in and eat with him, and he with Me" (Rev. 3:20). While this passage is not an evangelistic call—but rather a call of repentance to lukewarm, hardened Christians—the point remains that Jesus is willing to come to our door to sell us on a relationship with Him.

Make no mistake; every Christian is called to influence people with the gospel. We are all witnesses and, therefore, sellers of the Good News to anyone who will believe. The apostle Paul describes our call to sales in Second Corinthians 5:20, "We are therefore Christ's ambassadors, as though God were making His appeal through us. We implore you on Christ's behalf: Be reconciled to God." So, in a sense, the Church is God's worldwide, door-to-door sales force.

GREED-BASED CULTURE OF SALES VERSUS KINGDOM CULTURE OF SALES

Most people have a problem with sales and salespeople because most salespeople have been primarily influenced from the perspective and motivation of greed, which is reflective of the core value of the kingdom of darkness. How many of us have been swindled, scammed, talked into buying things we did not want, or seduced into lifestyles that seemed innocent but resulted in destruction and despair? That is exactly what Adam and Even experienced as the devil tempted them through a tantalizing sales pitch to eat of the forbidden fruit promising a better quality of life.

The devil used deceptive lies, masked manipulation, and relentless pressure to influence (sell) Adam and Eve. His motivation was selfish greed. He wanted the worship that he was not able to obtain in Heaven, so he continued to pitch his lower-level marketing scheme until he found some buyers. He was not interested in the least with Adam and Eve's welfare, or the quality of the product of enlightenment he was offering them. He also had no refund policy, and the customer service vanished after the papers were signed (see Gen. 3:1-19).

How many of us have been duped by salespeople who have sold us things that are now sitting in our garage waiting to be pawned off at the next garage sale at five cents on the dollar? No wonder so many people are leery of strangers approaching them with the opportunity of a lifetime. All too often the free lunch is followed by a lifetime commitment to payments of $39.95. It makes sense, then, why so many are skeptical of the "good news" we are attempting to present.

Unfortunately, most of us have encountered a greed-based culture of sales in the transactions that we have experienced. A greed-based culture of sales asks, "What can you do for me?" Whereas a Kingdom culture asks, "What can I do for you?" A greed-based culture demands, "You meet my needs." A Kingdom culture says, "I'll meet *your* needs." A greed-based culture thinks, "I'll do whatever it takes to manipulate you into buying." While a Kingdom culture of sales counters with "I will do anything to serve you."

You might be thinking to yourself right about now, "Boy, I have had plenty of Christians selling to me from the perspective of greed-based sales." Unfortunately that experience is too often true. Without even realizing it, many believers sell like the devil; they use the same manipulative, deceptive, and selfish tactics and motivation to coerce people into buying things that are regretted later. But that is just the way they were taught, as it almost seems like sales is a necessary evil that we must accept.

It does not have to be that way. Sales can be, and should be, very helpful and even a blessing to us. For that to be the case, however, we must recognize the huge difference between a Kingdom culture of sales and the greed culture of sales. While the devil's intention is to bring destruction and death in each transaction, God's purpose for influencing is to bless us.

The Kingdom culture of sales is best summed up in John 3:16, which says, "For God so loved the world that He gave His one and only Son, that whoever believes in Him shall not perish but have eternal life." Now that is a pretty good sales plan! Notice, God's motivation to influence is that He loved us and wants to bless us. The transaction is Jesus giving His life for our life, which is an amazing deal for us. The currency required to purchase "eternal life" is faith, which is something all of us have capacity for.

Moreover, once the transaction is complete in the Kingdom culture of sales, the desired goal is that both parties would have won, that both parties are blessed. In other words, when God attempts to influence us it is for our good *and* His. God never sells out of selfishness, but desires our benefit, and when we trust His intentions enough to believe, He is blessed because He gets us.

Most people have a hard time trusting God because they are so used to being influenced by a culture of greed—the kingdom of darkness. Therefore, it becomes difficult to believe God really does have our best interests in mind when He asks us to do things that we do not fully understand or desire. Those who have been scammed by other salesmen in the past are always looking for the hidden selfish agenda, even when it comes to trusting God. But God truly wants our best.

SALES IS SERVICE

Jesus stated His purpose succinctly in Mark 10:45, "For even the Son of Man did not come to be served, but to serve, and to give His life as a ransom for many." The epitome of the Kingdom culture of sales is service. The Greek word used in this passage for "serve" is *diakoneo*, which means "to minister." It is the same Greek word from which we get the term "deacon," one who is assigned to serve the church in practical ways. Specifically, *diakoneo*, to serve, means to meet someone's needs no matter what it is. Service is at the heart of the Kingdom culture of sales.

Therefore, as we have been commissioned to influence the world through service, our approach is to be one of meeting needs, serving in every way. The way Jesus served was to heal the sick, raise the dead, cast out demons, feed multitudes, turn water into wine, calm storms, and forgive prostitutes and tax collectors. He gave His time, energy, resources, and His very life for this purpose.

In Philippians 2:4-5, the apostle Paul exhorts us with these words, "Each of you should look not only to your own interests, but also to the interests of others. Your attitude should be the same as that of Christ Jesus...." In other words, we are to serve people in the same way Jesus did, by meeting whatever need they may have. This is a basic Kingdom sales principle.

Supernatural service is the heart of the Treasure Hunt as well. We are not going out to argue people into the Kingdom or manipulate them into joining our church. No, our goal is to demonstrate the goodness and kindness of God by meeting their needs, whether it is by giving them an encouraging word about their true identity and destiny, healing their body, or just listening as a friend. Effective Treasure Hunting is all about service.

Once they believe and receive the message in response to a practical demonstration, it is much easier for them to be added to the Church. We find this principle at work in the first evangelistic outreach of the newborn Church in Acts 2:41 when Peter addressed a large crowd on the Day of Pentecost. We are told that, "Those who accepted his message were baptized, and about three thousand were added to their number that day." Notice, it was only after they accepted the message through a demonstration that they joined the Church.

I'll never forget the time a friend and I were taking a walk when we noticed a moving truck. A young couple was struggling with some heavy furniture. They were shocked when we volunteered our help. Thirty minutes later, they accepted Jesus into their lives because we had earned their trust through service. We saw a need and took advantage of the opportunity to serve in a practical way. They ended up going to church with their next-door neighbor, and two more people were added to the Kingdom.

I NEED MANY OF THOSE BOOKS

I was leading a mission's trip to Tepic, Mexico, in which we were providing medical services to the indigenous Indian villages. The Lord gave me a strategy to set up a "waiting room," comprised of folding chairs on a patch of dirt under a shade tree. As the people came to the makeshift medical clinic to see the doctor, they were directed to the "waiting room" where several teams of our students and interpreters were waiting to release divine healing. Medicines are good and useful, but we found that miraculous healings serve the needs of the people even better.

One day, as we were conducting the medical clinic, a man in his forties came toward us walking like a penguin, his feet and arms awkwardly curling out from his body. The man grimaced in pain as he slowly made his way over to the clinic. He expressed that he needed medication to ease the pain because of the arthritis that riddled his body. We directed him to the "waiting room," where a team began to pray for him. A minute later, the man's grimace turned to joy as he started jumping up and down completely healed and pain free. After meeting his need, the team easily led the man to Christ.

The man bypassed the nurse and doctor at the medical table and went directly to our prophetic booth, where we were calling out the destiny of those who had received medical attention and/or been healed. As the man heard the prophecies about the plans and purposes God had for his life, he looked over at the interpreter and asked for some of the "books" (the Bible) that were being used for some of the prophetic words being given.

The interpreter told the man that he would get him one of the books, but the man replied, "No, I need many of those books." When asked why he would need more than one of the Bibles, the man replied, "Because I am the witch doctor of the village, and I can no longer teach the people to trust in the gods I have been declaring. I must begin to teach them about the God I have encountered today."

We went back to the same area a year later, but did not go to that same village. As we passed by, our guide explained that we were no longer needed in that village because everyone had believed in the Lord since our last visit; we were no longer needed! We had demonstrated our service in practical and supernatural acts, which granted us favor and enabled us to influence them to receive Christ.

The point of the Treasure Hunt is to convince people that they are God's Treasure that God is searching for them through us. If we are going to be able to uncover these hidden Treasures, however, it is essential that we gain favor in order to be able to influence them toward Christ. The way we do that is through practical acts of service, by meeting their needs according to the power that works within us (see Eph. 1:19). Remember, people do not care what you know until they know that you care. And they know that you care when you serve them the way Jesus served wherever He went.

A Picture Is Worth a Thousand Words—A Smile Gets Them to Listen

Finding the clues on your Treasure Map does not ensure that you will have a successful encounter. Most people are going to be suspicious when you initially approach them with the good news that they are your Treasure. That is why the first impression you make is the most important. And remember, you only have one chance at a first impression. Studies I have read and personal experience both indicate that the first ten seconds will determine whether or not you will be granted permission to continue.

A smile is like the gift of hospitality; it invites people into your world, so that they invite you into their world. A timely, genuine smile can go miles in making people feel comfortable. Christians could learn a great deal from the movie *Patch Adams.* In the movie, Patch is a medical student who realizes that if he could just get people to smile, or better yet, to laugh, then they would be more apt to trust him, resulting in his being able to better help them. The best way for you to know whether you are gaining favor with someone is if you get a return smile. The best way to get them to smile is to smile.

I remember one time I was laughing with myself in my car. I was stopped at a red light, and looked over at the woman in the car next to me. Without knowing what I was laughing about, she began to laugh with me through the closed windows. If the light had not turned green, I really think I could have led her to Christ because of the instant rapport we had in a common laugh. There have been so many times I have disarmed even the most hardened cynic with a smile, and as a result, gained entrance into his life for a divine appointment.

I was leading a Firestorm team down to Southern California, when we stopped for gas. The team piled out of the van and spontaneously gathered between the gas pumps to "drink." I was pumping gas while the students from the School of Supernatural Ministry were caught up in a laughing spree. I looked over at the adjacent pump and noticed a man smiling as he was watching the students. At that moment, the man and one of our students met eyes.

Our student asked the man, "Do you want some of this?" Without hesitation, he just nodded. "Do you know what this is?" the student followed. The man shook his head. The student invited the man over, and the team led him to Christ right between the gas pumps! The man was immediately filled with the Spirit and left laughing.

"You Had Me At Hello"

In order to be effective in Treasure Hunting, we have to have more than a smile; the smile opens the door, but our initial greeting captures their attention. I love the scene in the movie *Jerry Maguire*, when Jerry is trying to convince his wife to reconcile with him. He is going on and on about his change of heart, begging really hard. In the middle of his appeal, she interrupts and says, "Stop, just stop. You had me at hello."

When approaching someone during a Treasure Hunt, it is important to smile, but your "hello" will set the tone for your encounter. When I approach a potential Treasure, I like to say something that lets them know I understand how awkward it is to have someone enter their private space in public. I know how I feel when I am in a hurry and on task, and someone wants to take my time with the deal of the century. If they do not convince me to listen in the first sentence or two, I will politely excuse myself and turn a deaf ear to whatever may follow, until I can escape.

I have used a lot of opening greetings to initiate the divine appointment, but the most effective is to say, "Hi there. This may sound weird, but I'm on a Treasure Hunt, and I think you are on my Treasure Map." I like this greeting because it often makes them ask the question: "What is a Treasure Hunt?" to which you then have the opportunity to explain that God has highlighted them to you in order to help them or encourage them in some way.

BUILDING RAPPORT

If they ask the question, you have their attention; they are engaged. That is the time to show them the Treasure Map that you have been holding in their view during your greeting. It is important to point out each clue so that it sinks in that they truly are the Treasure you have been looking for. They will usually say something like, "This is crazy!" or "I can't believe this!" to which you can respond, "I know, it seems a little strange to me also, but there is no way I could have known this stuff about you without God's help." They will usually follow with "I know," followed by another question in search of an explanation to this unusual encounter. At that point you have connected; you are building rapport, as you are both standing there dumbfounded at the thought that God has indeed given you specific clues to find them.

At some point in the initial greeting and explanation, it is important to get on a first name basis. This can be achieved by asking if her name is "Cassandra" as you initially greet her, which immediately grabs her attention because you have never met her before, or by saying something like, "By the way, my name is Kevin, what is yours?" It is also good to extend your hand in a friendly gesture. If she accepts your hand, then you have built more rapport; your interaction has become personal.

I learned the importance of the smile, the name, and the handshake from a friend many years ago. Wherever we would go, he would greet some stranger with a great big smile, say his name, and hold out his hand. Sometimes he would hold out his hand for five seconds, which seemed like an eternity to me, but often, the person would eventually comply. Once he had his/her hand, he would hold on to it until he was finished saying how much God loved him/her. That approach may be a little too bold for many, but the idea is to connect as personably as possible. My friend led many people to Christ because of his boldness and genuine personal touch toward people.

OVERCOMING OBJECTIONS

Of course, there are going to be those who remain skeptical or even cynical toward any thought that God has highlighted them, not to mention admitting they may have a need for Him. Many reject God because they have had negative encounters in the past with Christians who have misrepresented God to them. Others are skeptical or cynical because they have lived so long without God that they just honestly do not think they need any help, or that none is available. Still others may be bitter because they asked God for something at some point and did not get the answer they were hoping for.

Unfortunately, most people who are not in the Church have a misconception of Christ and the Kingdom. Similarly, a lot of people in the Church have a wrong conception of the Kingdom, which unfortunately, they have presented to nonbelievers, making it that much harder to connect. It is our job, then, to represent the Father's heart in such a way that demonstrates His goodness and kindness in our words and deeds.

In order to demonstrate the goodness and kindness of God, however, we have to break through the barriers of resistance, and we do that by building rapport and overcoming objections. I have had people tell me that they do not believe in God after hearing an explanation of the Treasure Hunt. When that happens, my response has often been, "Well, He believes in you, and He has highlighted you today to let you know it. So what do you think about that?" And then I attentively listen, trying to discern the underlying objections that are preventing them from *buying* the Good News.

I love the scene in the movie, *Secondhand Lions*, when the salesmen are trying to tempt two brothers, retired treasure hunters, into spending their millions of dollars—which is stuffed away in the barn. As each salesman approaches the isolated Texas farm, they are filled with great anticipation over the big sale they are going to make. Each salesman, however, is met by shotgun pellets flying over his head and turns away before he even has a chance at a greeting.

But these two brothers have a problem. They are bored. They have lived great and exciting adventures, but now there is nothing for them to do but sit on their porch all day, sipping iced tea, waiting for a salesman to come along—for target practice. But that is no longer enjoyable because they are obviously not allowed to actually shoot their moving targets.

Finally, an astute salesman finds a way to solve their problem. He pulls up and convinces the bored men to give him one chance to prove he has something they want. He begins to describe the contraption hitched to the back of the car. The brothers had no idea as to its use. Without any explanation, he pulls out a shotgun of his own, directs the brother's young nephew to release the lever, and proceeds to shatter a clay pigeon as it soars through the sky. Without hesitation, they respond, "We'll take it." They do not even ask the price. Why? Because they have found something that has reignited their sense of passion and adventure.

Selling is simply asking yourself the question: "What are they buying?" Once the need is identified, it is simply a matter of meeting that need. I want to suggest that people are willing to buy into the Good News once they see that Jesus wants to fulfill their dreams and desires. We overcome objections by demonstrating the supernatural through practical acts of service, thus revealing the goodness and kindness of God that leads them to repentance (see Rom. 2:4).

POP THE QUESTION

Many years ago, I worked in high-end retail sales. I will never forget a guy who was hired who had the potential of being the top salesman in the company. He was great with people, immediately making connections and building rapport. He knew every detail of the product line and held the interest of the customer the entire time; he was a great communicator. His only problem, which turned out to be his downfall, was that he never asked for the order; he would never pop the question. Consequently, he hardly ever sold anything and eventually went into banking.

One day, I asked him why he did not simply ask the customer to buy the product he had spent so much time and energy presenting. His reply was that he was afraid they would say "No." So, he would just keep presenting until they either begged him for the product or finally left to "think about it." His fear of rejection prevented him from excelling in selling. Fear ultimately led him into a safer position, where he also settled for a significantly lower earning potential.

The most successful Treasure Hunters take the greatest risk. While Treasure Hunting I have had countless people say "No." Yet, in all honesty, receiving those negative responses is worth it if it means that I get even one "Yes." Sure, I have been rejected, but I have learned to embrace rejection as a friend, knowing that each encounter has hidden significance. The more I believe in the power of the Good News and who God has made me to be, the less I fear the rejection of man.

Often, the only thing preventing people from having an encounter is that you haven't yet popped the question, whether it is to pray for healing, blessing, encouragement, comfort, or to invite Christ into their heart. Once they have seen the demonstration, once you have built rapport, there is only one thing left: Pop the question! You really have nothing to lose and everything to gain. Moreover, you just may find the Ultimate Treasure!

CHAPTER 7

Essential Treasure-Hunting Equipment: Supernatural Divine Healing

❦

WHILE TREASURE HUNTING IN MIAMI, FLORIDA, our team was led to a hardware store with several clues such as "rakes," "hat," "Cuban," and "wrist." We found the "rakes" and waited. Just about the time we were deciding to give up on the *rake* location, a *Cuban* family turned up looking for a *rake*. Immediately, we noticed the father had a *hat* on and a *wrist* brace. One of the team members approached him but was interrupted by his wife who explained that her husband did not speak English.

As we began to explain that God had highlighted her husband to us, and how God wanted to heal his wrist, she became visibly skeptical and promptly told us that her family was Catholic. She added that he had just received a steel rod in his wrist making it permanently stabilized.

Consequently, she concluded, he was on disability and nothing further could be done about the wrist.

Without hesitation, one of the other team members inquired as to whether or not her husband had any pain associated with the recent surgery. "Oh yes!" she responded. "He is on pain medication." The team member went on to ask if we could just pray to reduce the pain. Apprehensively, she approved, and without her explaining to him our intentions, we gathered around and began to release the presence of God on him.

As we spoke to the pain, commanding it to leave and began releasing the *shalom* peace of God, the man broke into an ear-to-ear smile and then started crying. Troubled, his wife questioned him for a few minutes, and finally reported with a stunned expression that all of the pain had left his wrist. Meanwhile, the man had gone back to smiles, while his wife and kids stood dumbfounded.

After a few moments of silence, I jumped in and explained that God was healing him and asked her to tell him to remove the brace, which she did. With the brace now removed, we instructed her to have him move his wrist around. He looked confused, as though something was lost in translation. She repeated the request, and he began to move his wrist, bending it up and down. His face turned to utter shock upon seeing that he had complete mobility of the very wrist he was not supposed to be able to move.

Seeing that he had just been healed, his wife broke into tears and repeatedly thanked us for helping her husband. She went on and on about how they had been so distraught over the loss of income due to the disability, and how that her husband could now go back to work. Meanwhile, he continued to move his wrist around in every direction, carefully observing every movement like a child discovering a new toy.

We went on to explain how God had done this miracle for them because He cared about them and had a plan for their lives. We spoke about how God wanted to have a personal relationship with each one of them. They expressed that while they had been Catholics their whole lives, they had never known God in the personal way that we had demonstrated and discussed. So, right there in the hardware store, next to the "rakes," we had the privilege of leading this Cuban family of five to Christ.

Through the demonstration of a miraculous healing, this family discovered that they were God's Treasure. Supernatural divine healing is an essential tool for digging up hidden Treasure. Therefore, to have successful Treasure-Hunting expeditions, it is imperative that we value this Kingdom resource and learn to utilize it to its full potential.

HEALING IS A NORMAL EXPRESSION OF THE KINGDOM

Healing is meant to be a normal part of the Christian's arsenal in demonstrating the Kingdom of God. In Matthew 10:7-8, Jesus says, "*As you go, preach this message: 'The kingdom of heaven is near.' Heal the sick....*" The instruction in this passage is to preach and do; healing is an integral part of demonstrating that the Kingdom of God is near. Therefore, healing is an essential tool for the Treasure Hunter who is attempting to convince someone to believe the message.

Healing is a normal expression of the Kingdom of God. All throughout the Scriptures, there are promises and testimonies of God providing healing. In Exodus 15:26, God says, "I am the Lord, who heals you [Yahweh/Jehovah Rapha]." In Isaiah 53:4-5, we find the promise of Jesus' atoning sacrifice not only covering our sins but also our sickness. Jesus healed the sick to demonstrate the arrival of the Kingdom of God. In Matthew 4:23, we are told that, "Jesus went throughout Galilee...preaching the good news of the kingdom, and healing every disease and sickness among the people."

In John 20:21, after the resurrection, Jesus informed His disciples of their mission. He said, "As the Father has sent Me, I am sending you." Jesus sent out His disciples to demonstrate the Kingdom just as *He* had through healings, miracles, and signs and wonders. We then find demonstrations of miraculous healings throughout the Book of Acts, as the disciples/apostles and others utilized supernatural divine healing in proclaiming the Good News.

THERE IS MORE TO A NAME THAN JUST A NAME

A primary key to releasing the healing power of God is found in the story of Peter healing the crippled beggar in Acts 3. After healing the man, Peter addresses the on-looking crowd, explaining the source of the power to provide the cure. In verse 16, he points out, "It is Jesus' name and the faith that comes through Him that has given this complete healing to him, as you can all see" (Acts 3:16). The key to bringing healing into people's lives is the name of Jesus.

Regrettably, some people have been misled into the notion that as long as they put the phrase "in Jesus' name" as a tag to their request, whatever they have asked will be done. Some wield this phrase as though it is a lucky rabbit's foot: "If I just say 'in Jesus' name,' then it will happen." But it is important to understand that a *name* is more than a *name* in the Scriptures.

As mentioned, healing (*Yahweh/Jehovah Rapha*) is one of the many names used to reveal God (see Exod. 15:26). In the Bible, especially the Old Testament, a name signified a person's nature, character, personality, and attributes leading to predictable behaviors. Whatever name was used to identify God depicted a specific aspect of His divine nature, character, personality, and attributes. This principle not only applies to God, but to others as well.

For example, the name *Jacob* means "deceiver." Throughout his life we find him expressing his name through his behavior. In Genesis 27, Jacob deceives his brother Esau, cheating Esau out of his blessing, so that he has to flee to his uncle Laban's house. While taking refuge there, he uses deceptive tactics to steal Laban's sheep, forcing him once again to flee (see Gen. 30-31).

Even Jacob's sons, Simeon and Levi, followed in his deceptive conduct when Dinah, their sister, was abused by the Shechemites. Simeon and Levi offered impunity to them if they agreed to circumcision. Once they submitted to the procedure, however, they were killed, even though a promise had been given (see Gen. 34).

Now, back in Genesis 32, Jacob has a wrestling match with God, which ends in Jacob being blessed with a name change. In verse 28, God says, "Your name will no longer be Jacob, but Israel, because you have struggled with God and with men and have overcome." The implication is that, in overcoming, Jacob became *blessed.*

God confirms Jacob's new identity in Genesis 35:10, saying, "'Your name is Jacob, but you will no longer be called Jacob; your name will be Israel.' So He named him Israel (He who struggles with God and wins, or Blessed)." In reading the rest of Israel's history throughout the Old Testament, we find the nation of Israel struggling with God, and even in their rebellion they ultimately won with God and were blessed. Even today, God is working towards blessing the Jews even through hardship and persecution. Israel is their name. Therefore, they cannot help but to be blessed; it is their identity.

Along the same line, among the many names used to describe the enemy, the name *devil* means "divider." The Greek word is *diaballo*, which means to throw a ball through the middle of something (*dia* = through; and *ballo* = ball), and subsequently, to divide.

Division is what the devil does; it is who he is, and you see the effects of his name everywhere. His name is a reflection of his nature, character, personality, and attributes. To accomplish his will, the devil uses miscommunication, offenses, and other divisive tactics to separate what God has joined together. Divorce and church splits are always the will of the devil. I am not saying that a person never has the scriptural right to divorce or discontinue a relationship in various contexts, but even so, it still grieves the heart of God when a family is split apart due to adultery or abuse, and when people cannot get along in a church or a business situation.

Similarly, whenever we find a revelation of God's name in Scripture, it is an expression of His nature, character, personality, and attributes leading to predictable behavior. His name is who He is. His name is what He does and how He acts; His name is His very nature. So then, if His name is Healer, it means that healing is part of His nature, expressed through His behavior. That is why we can never say that God wants someone to be, or remain, physically sick or crippled. God is Healer; it is who He is, and therefore what He always desires.

HALLOWED BE YOUR NAME

In the prayer Jesus taught His disciples to pray in Matthew 6:9-12, He began by teaching them to pray, "Our Father in Heaven, hallowed be Your name." The word *hallowed* is also translated "holy" in some of our English translations and means "consecrated, sanctified, or set apart." When we say, "hallowed be Your name," we are saying that His nature, character, personality, and attributes are unlike any other earthly expression. In other words, nothing compares with our Father in Heaven.

It is similar to the difference between Spam and filet mignon. Our Father in Heaven is like perfectly seasoned and cooked filet mignon. Conversely, even the best father on earth is like Spam in comparison. Some people love Spam; it is all they have ever tasted. Some choose to eat Spam because they cannot afford filet mignon, and so, have adjusted their taste accordingly. I have tasted both and have unequivocally concluded that filet mignon is *hallowed*; it is set apart, consecrated, and holy. Nothing, especially Spam, can compare with filet mignon; it is on a whole different level.

So it is with the name of our Father. His nature, character, personality, and attributes are above anything of this world. So when we pray, "Our Father in Heaven, hallowed be Your name," we are praying that everything that expresses His name be revealed, so that people see that He is incomparable to anything else available. Healing, *Yahweh/Jehovah Rapha*, is just one of the many aspects of our Father's name that reflects His greatness.

ON EARTH AS IN HEAVEN

Bill Johnson, in his book, *When Heaven Invades Earth*, astutely points out that God could never *will* sickness. In Matthew 6:9, Jesus taught us to pray, "Your kingdom come, Your will be done, on earth as it is in Heaven." Therefore, since there is no cancer in Heaven, it is God's will that there be no cancer here on earth. There is no division, anxiety, abuse, hatred, or unforgiveness in Heaven either, which means God's desire, His will, is that none of those things are allowed to exist on the earth.

But not everyone is healed. True, but it is still God's *will* that they are healed. Not everyone is saved, but it is God's will that no one perish (see 2 Pet. 3:9). It may be that God's will is not in question, but our ability to bring the Kingdom of God into this earthly realm is. At Bethel Church, we are learning to access what is in Heaven and bring it back to earth.

Recently, one of our School of Supernatural Ministry students was part of a team ministering at a church in Santa

Rosa, California. A woman was limping through an impartation tunnel that the students had formed to release empowerment for signs and wonders to those going through. As this 72-year-old student watched the woman laboring through the tunnel, she was prompted to pull her aside to minister to her.

When asked to explain the reason for the limp, the woman shared that she had been in a car accident two years prior, and as a result, the doctors had to remove her kneecap. The reason the woman was limping was that she had no kneecap. Unfazed, the ministry school student told the woman to wait for a moment while she went to Heaven to get a new kneecap.

She lifted up her hand and grabbed what seemed to be air. She then placed her hand on the woman's knee. Immediately, the woman began to exclaim that she had received a new kneecap as she ran through the crowd completely healed. This breakthrough came as a result of somebody taking responsibility to bring Heaven to earth. Each one of us has the capability and responsibility to bring supernatural divine healing to people, revealing the goodness and kindness of God through the power of His name.

I Might Kill You

I used to have 100 percent success in healing; everyone I prayed for was healed. The catch is: I didn't pray for anyone, so no one ever got healed. During the first three years of my Christian life, however, I had prayed for many people and several were healed. One day I was called on to pray for a woman who had cancer. I went full of faith and prayed for the woman, fully expecting her to improve. That night, however, I found out she had died shortly after I prayed for her. I was devastated. I was overcome with the idea that I had killed her because I really did not have a gift of healing and should have summoned the assistance of someone who did.

I spent the next 23 years avoiding praying for the sick. I believed in healing, and I believed that the Kingdom of God could break into this earthly realm. I just did not believe that I could administrate the grace of healing because I did not have the gift. As a pastor, if I knew of someone who was sick, I would call on one of the *gifted ones* in the church. I would often quip, "You don't want me to pray for you. I might kill you!"

I truly believed people were better served if I did not pray for them. Then, one day the Lord got my attention with a question: "Kevin, do you really believe you have the power to cause someone to die?"

"No, Lord. Of course not," I responded.

"Then you do not have the power to heal someone either," He countered.

I got the point.

YOU HAVE WHAT IT TAKES: CHRIST IN YOU, THE HOPE OF GLORY

Our job is to bring God's Kingdom to earth, which means that we represent His name in our lives. We are called Christians because we have taken His name. We are the children of God (see 1 John 3:1), which means we are to be identified with His name. Therefore, we have the power associated with the Name we carry, in order to meet any need we encounter.

Not only do I have His name, but Christ also lives in me to live through me. In Colossians 1:27, Paul says that it is "Christ in you, the hope of glory." Therefore, I have what it takes to reveal the glory of God through my life. Jesus said in Luke 17:21, "The kingdom of God is within you." God is simply looking for those who will release what is inside of them.

I cannot save anyone, but Christ in me can save everyone. I cannot deliver anyone, but Christ in me can deliver everyone. Similarly, I cannot heal anyone, but Christ in me can heal everyone. Giving the Kingdom away is simply giving away the Jesus inside of us. Of course, in one sense, I have as much of Christ as I will ever get, but in another sense, there is still more of Him being formed in me (see Gal. 4:19). So then, the more Christ is formed in me, the more I will have to give away. The ministry of healing is simply releasing the presence of Christ that is residing within us.

My breakthrough in understanding this principle came in January 2001. We had a young man living with us at the time who had been disabled for three months due to a ruptured disk in his lower back while at work. He had just gone through surgery, but had not been helped. He was left bedridden, and in constant pain. I felt horrible, watching him suffering in so much pain, without my being able to help him.

One night, as we were preparing for a fellowship group in our home, he asked for a few of the guys from the group to help him out to the couch where he could lay down to participate with us and take his mind off the pain. He writhed in pain throughout the meeting, however, and ultimately became the focus of the meeting. Finally, he pleaded with me to pray for God to heal him.

Reluctantly, I succumbed to his desperate plea. I figured his condition could not get any worse, and besides, there was no one else in the room who had the gift. So, I was the best option available. I instructed the guys who had brought him out to the couch to stand him up. I went to him and hesitantly placed my hand on his back. I was just about ready to launch into a *comforting* prayer, to help him in his suffering, but before I could, he yelled out, "Do you feel that fire on my back where your hand is?" To my amazement, my hand felt like it was on fire, and I had not even prayed!

A few moments later, he bent over, and then jumped high in the air and exclaimed, "This is amazing! All of the pain is gone; I am healed!" He continued, "This is amazing…this is amazing!" and then started crying, as he continued to jump around our living room demonstrating his complete healing. At one point, he sat down on the couch, looked up at me with tears of joy, and then jumped off the couch into a flying karate kick.

I was shocked. First, because he was healed as I had placed my hand on his back, and second, because my hand was still on fire, even though it was no longer on his back. Knowing this was a *God thing*, I asked if anyone else needed to be healed. Two others immediately responded, and as I placed my hand on them, they were instantaneously healed. In the process, I understood that healing is not necessarily about gifting, but the released manifest presence of God—Christ in me, the hope of glory.

I often travel to churches, activating them in supernatural divine healing. One of the common misconceptions I encounter is that healing is a matter of learning all of the techniques and formulas to increase effectiveness. They often expect me to offer them a ten point "how to" on getting people healed. While principles can facilitate breakthrough, I have found that physical healing is more a matter of releasing His presence.

Of course, there are those who see a lot of people healed utilizing techniques they have learned from someone else who fought for a breakthrough by praying in a certain way, but often I will use a technique that brought healing breakthrough in the past, only to find it ineffective, even though all of the factors were exactly the same as before. I have learned that the common denominator in getting people healed is His glorious presence released through faith.

This Is My Son

Another key I have acquired in releasing physical healing is living and operating in the truth of son-ship. In Matthew 3:17, while Jesus is being baptized by John the Baptist, the Holy Spirit descends upon Him, and the Father speaks audibly from Heaven saying, "This is My Son, whom I love; with Him I am well pleased." This statement is a public declaration of Jesus' identity: "This is My Son...."

Before this event, there are no records of Jesus demonstrating supernatural ministry. It was not until He was baptized, received the Spirit, and heard the pronouncement from His Father that He performed His first miracle of turning water into wine while at Cana (see John 2:11). Peter, in Acts 10:38, explained that it was the anointing of the Spirit that enabled Jesus to heal. But I want to propose that the words of the Father spoken here in Matthew 3:17 were just as crucial to releasing the supernatural kingdom through Jesus' life.

In Jewish tradition, it was customary for a father to bring his eldest son to a public place (normally the city gates where business and judicial decisions were transacted), put his arm around him, and proclaim to the "powers that be" that his son now had authority to transact family business on his behalf. Upon that declaration, the son had full rights to buy or sell anything in the family business as if the father were conducting the transaction himself. From that point on, he had full authority and empowerment as a son.

In the same way, at Jesus' baptism, the Father speaks from Heaven and proclaims to the world that His Son, Jesus, is now authorized to transact Kingdom business on His behalf. Not only does He have empowerment through the Holy Spirit, but also authority through His recognized identity as a son. I would suggest that many Christians, who have been empowered by the Holy Spirit, have been frustrated in healing the sick because of their lack of understanding of the son-ship/daughter-hood they enjoy with the Father.

In John 15:15-17, Jesus, speaking to His disciples, says, "I no longer call you servants, because a servant does not know his master's business. Instead, I have called you friends...and appointed you to go and bear fruit—fruit that will last. Then the Father will give you whatever you ask in My name." In this dialogue, the disciples received an upgrade; they have been elevated from servants to friends. And then, later in the New Testament, the revelation of the status of their relationship is elevated to that of children—sons and daughters (see 1 John 3:1; Rom. 8:12-17).

Bill Johnson and Kris Vallotton, in their books and teachings, have often pointed out that the way we operate in the Kingdom is essentially based upon how we view our identity. Having a proper revelation of our identity determines the level of Kingdom authority we walk in, which will determine the amount of influence we have in bringing the Kingdom of God to earth. I found this concept especially true as it relates to getting breakthrough in physical healing.

Living as God's *children* gives us confidence that we can access Heaven whenever we desire to get whatever we want. We also become cognizant of the authority we have, as royal sons and daughters, to release on earth what we have accessed in the Kingdom of God. Based upon the view of our identity as children, then, we are able to enjoy a deeper sense of intimacy, which in turn, releases a greater measure of confidence in releasing Kingdom authority.

It is out of this place of intimacy that I understand it is His good pleasure to give me the Kingdom (see Luke 12:32). Healing, then, being a revelation of His Name and, therefore, the will of God and His Kingdom, is released in and through me from intimacy. In other words, as a son, I am a carrier of His glory through the intimate relationship I have with Him. While on a Treasure Hunt, I simply release that which I have accessed in His presence.

Learning to live as a son has helped me grow in confidence as I encounter those who need a miracle in their body. I have come to know that I have what it takes to broker God's Kingdom, because I know that I am a son. I have heard the words for myself: "This is my son...." As a result, I have become more convinced that the Father has specifically given me the keys to the Kingdom and has commissioned me to transact Kingdom business on His behalf (see Matt. 16:19). Healing, therefore, is not based on a certain gifting I might possess, but rather, is connected to my taking responsibility to be the Kingdom *business-man* He has identified as my identity.

CHAPTER 8

Essential Treasure-Hunting Equipment: Supernatural Prophetic Insights

L IKE HEALING, THE PROPHETIC is essential Treasure-Hunting equipment. Getting words of knowledge, finding the clues, taking risk, and even building rapport with the people we encounter are all important aspects of the Treasure Hunt. But sharing supernatural insights of God's thoughts regarding the people we meet often supplies the crucial key in opening their hearts to receive the Good News we are ultimately offering.

Many times, God provides us with prophetic insights as we initially write down the clues of our Treasure Maps. Often these prophetic clues are given as "marriage problems," "hopelessness," "grief," or some other obscure clue that will provide a launching point for the prophetic once we have engaged a potential Treasure. Most often, however, the prophetic is not premeditated, but emerges naturally in the course of conversation during an encounter.

I HAVE WHAT IT TAKES

I learned this principle several years ago when I was praying for a man named Steve during a ministry time after a church service. He had not given any details of what he wanted prayer for, other than that he really needed to hear from God regarding a crucial decision he needed to make.

I prayed for him as I normally did on these occasions; I focused on general prayers of comfort and encouragement in an attempt to give him hope that God would speak to him regarding the situation he was in, as well as the specific strategies to be able to work through the details of his particular circumstances. I went on to quote some Scriptures of God's faithfulness and His ability to provide for everything.

I finished praying, and Steve thanked me with no apparent evidence of anything significant having transpired, other than my communicating a sense of caring for a man who had needed some encouragement that God was with him. A few weeks later, however, he informed me that my *prophetic* prayer had provided the specific detailed answers for the decisions he needed to make that very day.

He told me that in the middle of my prayer, unbeknown to me, I had changed my address of him from "Steve" to "Stephen." He continued, saying that the Lord had audibly spoken to him a few times in the past, and had always addressed him as "Stephen." He also clarified that he had never referred to himself as "Stephen," and no one knew him by that name. So, when I *accidentally* started calling him "Stephen," it caught his attention. Without being aware, I prophesied the very solutions he needed, giving him the exact details he needed for the crucial decision he was under pressure to make.

Prior to this encounter, I had never considered myself a prophetic person, even though on occasion, as long as I felt an overwhelming unction, I could give someone a simple, general prophetic word with a certain amount of confidence. Candidly speaking, the prophetic people I had met were on the eccentric, and sometimes bizarre, side of the types of Christians I had encountered, even within the Pentecostal/Charismatic movement in which I had been associated since 1975.

Needless to say, I had never pursued prophetic ministry because I did not share those same eccentricities and did not want to be associated with those *strange* people who did. So, while I certainly believed in the prophetic, I did not think it was my gift or part of my calling and responsibility in demonstrating the Kingdom. Yet, the experience with Steve taught me that God wants to speak through me even when I am not consciously aware of His voice, that because I have the Kingdom inside of me, I have what it takes to be prophetic.

In our church culture at Bethel, especially modeled by Kris Vallotton, our senior associate pastor, we are learning to carry the prophetic everywhere we go, as well as looking for opportunities to utilize it in any encounter we have. For us, *speaking* God's will is just as important as *doing* God's will in bringing Heaven to earth. Therefore, we are aspiring to be a prophetic people in the normal course of our daily lives, as a natural, supernatural lifestyle.

I DON'T HAVE ONE, BUT I CAN GET ONE!

During Treasure Hunts, supernatural prophetic insights are utilized to reveal the secrets of the heart in order to convince the person that God specifically cares about him and has a good plan for his life (see 1 Cor. 14:24-25). The prophetic releases hope that the future will be brighter and blessed as they realize that God is in a good mood toward them. The prophetic, then, is simply being a conduit between the heart of God and the Treasure we are attempting to recover.

As with words of knowledge, growing in the use of the prophetic comes with practice and risk. Many Christians do not think they are able to prophesy unless they have a burning bush experience dictating the message they are to speak, word for word. Paul exhorts us, however, to eagerly desire prophecy (see 1 Cor. 14:1). In other words, prophecy is not an inherent attribute of our new nature, but a supernatural gift offered to every Christian, and must be developed through risk and practice.

A few years ago, we were in Lake Tahoe conducting a Treasure Hunt in early December. There was already snow covering the ground, and all of our clues were for outdoors. We had been on the Treasure Hunt for about an hour when we decided that enough was enough. We had briefly spoken to a few prospects, but none had panned out, so we decided to head back to the church before our allotted time for the Hunt was finished.

A little discouraged, and very cold, we came to a huge "digital clock" on the side of the road, which was on our Treasure Map. In spite of the freezing cold, we were encouraged enough by the clue to wait for a Treasure to arrive.

After a few minutes, it was obvious we were the only ones foolish enough to be hanging out at a digital clock while it was 24 degrees outside! Just when that notion came to us, and we had decided to give up, we noticed dolphins painted on the side of the adjacent building. That was unusual—first, because we were at Lake Tahoe and there are no dolphins in the lake, and second, because we had "dolphins" on our Treasure Map under the *unusual* category.

Knowing that our Treasure was probably waiting for us inside, I asked one of our School of Supernatural Ministry students, Israel, if he had a prophetic word for the person inside the business. His response was profound: "No, but I can get one!"

Sometimes we are waiting to happen upon the burning bush, while God is always inviting us to access His presence to get what we need for the moment. Israel's astute observation, standing in the cold by a digital clock, models the reality that the prophetic is always available for sons and daughters in the Kingdom.

We made our way into the business and noticed that a young woman was behind the counter waiting for a customer. Since no one else was in the store, we decided she was our Treasure. We approached her, explaining our reason for being in the store: We were there looking for Treasure. I then asked Israel to give her the prophetic word that he had (I hoped) obtained during the short walk into the shop.

He prophesied to her for several minutes, calling out her true identity and destiny. He went on to share some prophetic insights into some personal issues she was working through, providing hope for a breakthrough. He also prophesied words of blessing and financial breakthrough over the business. The young woman was amazed at how accurately Israel's prophetic words related to her life and the business she worked for.

A year later, I was in the same area having lunch at a sidewalk table outside of a café with the pastor of the church we had conducted the Treasure Hunt with the previous year. While eating, a man approached us to offer thanks for the people who had come into his business on a cold winter day, last December, and encouraged his employee and prayed for financial blessing over his business.

It turned out that the young woman we had prophesied to the year before had called the owner of the business as soon as we had left to let him know of our prayer of blessing, and how she felt totally released from hopelessness and depression. The man told us that her life had been radically changed that day, and that his business, which had been close to bankruptcy, had since had a complete turnaround and was now prospering.

This testimony came as a result of someone's tapping into the prophetic realm of the Kingdom of God and grabbing supernatural insights from the heart of the Father to be used to demonstrate His goodness and kindness. The prophetic was never intended to just be a Sunday morning public event, but a normal, everyday activity of the believer. I am advocating that the prophetic realm is always available to those who are willing to press in to what God is saying and doing.

THE PURPOSE OF PROPHECY

Throughout the Scriptures, there are two basic expressions of the prophetic. One is *foretelling* future events, and the other is *forth-telling* the will of God for a person or circumstance. Many have a problem with operating in the prophetic as a natural Kingdom lifestyle because they view prophecy from a *foretelling* perspective. Interestingly, most of the Old Testament prophecies are *forth-telling* God's will versus *foretelling* future events.

In First Corinthians 14:3, Paul teaches that the prophetic is primarily meant for "strengthening" or edification (also "building up" in verse 12), "encouragement" or exhortation, and "comfort." All of these outcomes are more in line with forth-telling God's heart for people and circumstances, revealing His will rather than future events.

Of course, the way we view God will determine the way we prophesy our perception of His will. For example, if we view Him as a condemning and judging Father, our prophetic messages will tend to focus on the sin and shortcomings of people. On the other hand, if we view God as a loving God who is always in a good mood toward us and always works toward redemptive solutions, then we will prophesy from that perspective.

Interestingly, Paul does not list "judgment" as one of the uses of the prophetic ministry in First Corinthians 14. He does not challenge us to call out people's sins and mistakes in order to get them to repent. Rather, in verses 24 and 25, he says that when we prophesy, "he will be convinced by all that he is a sinner and will be judged by all, and the secrets of his heart will be laid bare. So he will fall down and worship God, exclaiming, 'God is really among you!'"

Kris Vallotton, in his excellent prophetic manual, *Basic Training for the Prophetic Ministry*, gives this commentary of these verses. He says:

> Notice in this passage that the person who receives the prophetic word doesn't repent but rather "will fall on his face and worship God." ...Most people know what is wrong with them but they are unaware of the greatness that God has placed in their lives.... Prophecy brings people into a revelation of the glory that God has assigned to them. This exposure brings conviction in their lives that they are living below the glorious standard that God has set for them.[1]

The purpose of the prophetic, then, is to expose a person to her true identity and destiny, showing her that there is far more than what she is currently experiencing. Prophecy calls her into the prophetic potential that God has designed for her life, showing that God has planned something better.

CALLING OUT THE GOLD

People already know what is wrong with them; what they do not know is what is right about them. One does not necessarily need to be prophetic to discern that someone is in a crisis, in need of counseling, or bound in some way. Just about anyone can state the obvious: You have a problem. Conversely, prophetic insights are needed to provide the answers.

For five years during the 1980s, I worked for a company that represented Fortune 500 companies to the subsidiary Japanese car manufacturers located in Southern California. We were responsible for the coordination of the design, development, and manufacturing of original equipment products that were installed at various ports around the United States.

During my first year, I would sometimes enter one of the owner's offices to describe a problem that I had encountered while moving a certain project along. I would spend several minutes outlining the problem in full detail and give great insight as to why the problem existed. Each time, he would respond by asking if I had a solution to the problem. I would usually tell him that I had not been able to figure that out, which was the reason for coming into his office.

Finally, one day as I outlined a multimillion-dollar problem, an owner interrupted me, saying, "Kevin, you have an amazing grasp of the obvious! I know what the problem is; I am paying you to find the solutions!"

Although that may seem like a harsh way of getting someone's attention, I needed to hear the rebuke at the time, and the principle has stuck with me since. That revelation not only helped me in the business realm, but also helped me realize that I had given a lot of attention to finding the problems in people's lives and the Church without focusing on the solutions.

I began to adjust my focus from the problems to the solutions. From that point on, as I encountered problems, I would ask God to give me prophetic insight into the solutions. I began to ask for supernatural solutions and an outline of His redemptive purposes and prophetic potential for each person and circumstance.

Throughout the Scriptures, God was always prophesying the solution along with the obvious problem. He was always highlighting the prophetic potential of His people and the redemptive purposes that were in His heart to fulfill. The purpose of the prophetic is to call out the hidden glory, the missing identity, and the unfulfilled destiny. The prophetic finds the gold and calls it out. That is at the heart of the Treasure Hunt.

I HAVE HAD ENOUGH—FINDING GOLD THROUGH THE PROPHETIC

Sometimes it is difficult to see the prophetic possibilities in an encounter. In fact, many of the Treasures we have found did not initially look like Treasures. Through the years, I have found that just as God "spoke" and the world was created, so we have the ability to call forth that which we cannot see with our eyes and bring what is not into reality. The prophetic helps us to find the gold in people, when all of our focus may be on the dirt.

I had been conducting healing meetings in Miami over four days and was exhausted as I waited for my flight to board to take me home. I was also a little irritated because the flight was full, and the ticket agent had somehow not secured my aisle seat, which left me in a middle seat all the way back to California.

I waited to board and, with just a few minutes to spare, made my way down the aisle to my assigned seat...where I was greeted by a screaming baby and her mother in the window seat next to mine. My irritation level increased dramatically as I realized the implications of having changing altitudes added to this already unhappy baby. The aisle seat was empty, so I sat in it by faith, praying that the owner would not show up, giving me much needed grace after the long extended weekend of ministry.

I stared toward the entrance of the plane, willing the person not to show, while at the same time, out of the corner of my eye, seeing the mother and her wailing child and wondering if I could even survive the flight sitting one seat over. To make matters worse, the baby was lying in its mother's lap with its head hanging over into my assigned seat.

Just as I began to feel confident that the person in my refugee seat was not coming, two gypsies came onto the plane. The taller of the two slid into a seat toward the front, and my confidence resurged a little. The shorter gypsy kept walking, however, and as I frantically accounted for all of the remaining seats on the airplane, I realized that I was currently in the gypsy's seat.

The closer he came the more it became evident that he had not bathed in a long time. He had dreadlocks down to the middle of his back, accented with a full beard that hung in clumps from his face. He had an open-chested, puffy-sleeved shirt with strands of demonic looking necklaces hanging from his neck and circus-looking pants that were tight around the ankles and ballooned out toward his waist. He wore hemp sandals and carried a backpack and a *djembe* (a small hand drum). He looked like Charles Manson meets Mr. Homeless, meets Bob Marley, although he appeared more South American than Jamaican.

Over the next few seconds, I looked back and forth from the crying baby to the Manson gypsy. And then he stopped at my seat. I did not even have to ask. I unbuckled the seat belt that I had previously put on by faith and moved over to my middle seat where I was sandwiched between a wild-eyed, screaming little head and satan.

At that moment, I screamed as loud as I could, inside my head, shouting, *This is it! I am not going to take any more of this. I am going to release the justice of God into the atmosphere. I am going to preach the gospel to these people next to me all of the way to California whether they like it or not. And if they don't, they can leave!*

I turned to the woman next to me, introduced myself, and began prophesying over her baby. I started calling out his destiny, and then, proceeded to get a word of knowledge about a parent who was ill. She informed me that she was on her way home from visiting her father who had just suffered a heart attack and was still in the hospital. I began to prophesy things about his life that convinced her that God was getting her attention.

Within ten minutes we were like long-time friends. Her baby even stopped crying, which was the greatest miracle of the day. I began to inquire about her husband, at which time she began to cry, telling me that he was unemployed and was very discouraged about getting a job in his field. I began to prophesy specific things about his heart's desires and God's purpose to help him; her tears turned to relief.

We spent another ten minutes or so talking about God's plan for her life. She confessed that she was a Christian, but had not been going to church because of a recent move and her husband's depressed mood. When I asked if she would like me to pray with her, she readily agreed, and we prayed together for God's purposes to be fulfilled in her life and her family.

I then turned to the gypsy sitting in the coveted aisle seat and struck up a conversation with him even though he was engrossed in the novel, *The Da Vinci Code.* I began with, "It's interesting that you are reading that book about the journey of a man trying to find the truth about Jesus because you're about to have an encounter in which Jesus reveals Himself to you." He put the book down to inquire as to how I had determined his fate.

I explained that God often gives me insights for people to show them how much He cares about their life. He shrugged his shoulders, looking like he wanted to return to his book, but I continued: "You're like Thomas in the Bible. God is going to show up when you least expect it." His face turned to shock. He informed me that his name was Thomas, and that he had been on a one-year journey, traveling around the world searching for the true God.

He had never heard about the Thomas of the Bible, so I showed him the passage out of my Bible. His eyes grew larger with each word. When he was finished, he exclaimed, "That's me. This is crazy. How did you know my name was Thomas?" I explained that God knew his name and had just given me the idea of the story of Thomas. We spent the next four hours talking about everything of his life and God's good purposes for him.

As it turned out, he was the son of a millionaire and was a world-class athlete who had, two years prior, been a member of the Portuguese national rugby team. He said that he had left everything to find the truth about God. When we finally landed and disembarked from the airplane, he introduced me to his traveling partner, and we hugged like father and son. In the end, I did not get any sleep on that flight but instead had an encounter with three Treasures that made for a trip of a lifetime.

DESTINY RESCUES A FAMILY

We never know how our prophetic insights will impact someone's life. Often, while on Treasure Hunts, calling out people's destinies (the gold) provides the catalyst for change, enabling them to take hold of promises and blessings God has in store for their lives.

On one occasion, we tracked down a woman with a clue of "white turtleneck." The woman's turtleneck sweater was actually cream, but because it was about 80 degrees outside, we figured the color was close enough. We found her in the plumbing aisle of a large home improvement store, shopping there with her husband.

I approached the woman, showing her the "white turtleneck" clue, and even though it was not the exact color, the woman seemed to accept the slight discrepancy as she listened attentively to our explanation of the Treasure Hunt. I began to call out some of the other clues we had on our list, and then came to "gastro-intestinal." She gasped, and explained that she and her husband had just come from the hospital where her father had just gone through a second operation to cut out a tumor in his colon. The doctors had informed them that the tumor would most likely grow back again, and that they should prepare for the worst.

We were able to pray with the couple, who were very grateful that God had used us to track them down to comfort them in their time of grief. Once we had finished praying for the woman's father, I continued down my list. I came to "business problems," and the husband sunk down as he informed us that his father-in-law's illness had taken a financial toll on the business because of all of the time spent at the hospital over the previous year.

We began to prophesy about his business, outlining some of the strategies that could bring increase. His jaw dropped as he listened because he had just written down each of the insights the day before. We then prayed for him, blessing the various aspects of the business; we prayed that he would see the glory of the Lord in his business, and from that would also know that God cared about every detail of his life.

I noticed that during the 15 minutes we had been with this couple, they had been standing about three feet apart. Since I had "marriage problems" on my list, I began to explain how family illness and financial stress can adversely impact a marriage relationship. Immediately, the woman began to cry. With tears running down her face she confessed that although both of them were Christians, they had just discussed divorce after leaving the hospital.

A holy passion and boldness rose up in a young woman who was on our Treasure Hunting team, and she began prophesying over the couple. We could sense the heartbeat of God's heart as she pleaded with them to reconsider such a course of action and be reconciled. She then began to prophesy about the two children she did not know they had, calling out their destiny and the responsibility of this mom and dad to bring them into that destiny. She went on and on about the specific callings that both of the children had on their lives.

Finally, the husband moved over to his wife, and with tears flooding his eyes, asked his wife to forgive him for wanting to give up on their marriage. She in turn asked for forgiveness, and both were reconciled, which culminated in hugs and kisses as we watched the reunion of husband and wife. It was the prophetic that called out the gold in their children, and in their marriage that paved the way for a family to be redeemed from the divisive strategies of the evil one.

As we were finishing, I felt a tap on my shoulder. I turned around to find that it was one of the store employees. I thought we were going to be asked to discontinue our revival meeting in the aisle, when the employee announced, "I have never seen anything like this before. I have been standing within earshot the entire time, and I just want you to know that this is the most incredible thing I have ever seen!"

Over the years, we have uncovered many Treasures like the ones we found that day in the aisle of the home improvement store. It is amazing how people respond so profoundly as their God-ordained destiny is called out in their life, and how they are changed in one supernatural encounter.

I want to encourage you to take some risk and release the prophetic ministry residing within you because of the

Kingdom within you, which is Christ in you, the hope of glory.

ENDNOTE

1. Kris Vallotton, *Basic Training for the Prophetic Ministry*, (Shippensburg, PA: 2005) 13, 14.

CHAPTER 9

Essential Treasure-Hunting Equipment: Supernatural Measures of Faith

꜀꜀꜀꜀

F OR MOST PEOPLE, when they hear of going on a Treasure Hunt, the first emotion they feel is fear. The thought of approaching people they have never met is intimidating beyond comprehension for many. Surprisingly, it is at least a little bit like that for me each time as well. Think about it: The Greek word for "witness" is *martus*, from which we also get the English word "martyr." That means that every time we "witness," something is potentially going to die. Consequently, each time in preparation for a Treasure Hunt, I have to convince myself that the Ultimate Treasure is worth the risk and is only found through supernatural measures of faith.

On many occasions, I have watched specific clues on my Treasure Map walk by as I try to muster up enough courage to stop them. Often, I will track them down once I have conquered my fears and engage in an amazing divine encounter. Unfortunately, at other times, by the time I stir up my faith to step out, they are gone. I have come to realize that I need supernatural measures of faith as I pursue the Ultimate Treasure.

God has called us to the mission impossible: the great commission, making disciples of all nations. Therefore, if we plan on fulfilling what Jesus has commanded us to do, we must increase in supernatural measures of faith to enable the impossible to become possible. We must be able to take greater levels of risk if we hope to recover all of the Treasures hidden throughout the world. Faith is an essential piece of equipment for those who would become Ultimate Treasure Hunters.

"I'M GOING TO DIE"

During the summer when I was ten years old, my mother would sometimes take my friends and me to Surprise Lake, where they had a huge slide, a 3-foot diving board, and a tower that had a 10-, 20-, and 30-foot platform from which we kids could jump, or if we were very brave, could dive. At ten years old, I was not very brave. In fact, while my friends were jumping off of the 10-foot platform, I was very content with the lower level 3-foot diving board.

In my heart, I wanted to join my friends at the higher level, but my fear of heights kept me from taking the necessary risk. Meanwhile, I continued to "work on my form" off the diving board, while my friends soared with hoops and hollers off the 10-foot platform. They continued to call to me from the higher platform, assuring me that I could do it, that it was safe, and much more fun. Even though I could see that they were having fun, and were surviving the perilous leap, I, nonetheless, continued to feel like I would be the first to die jumping off of the tower.

My friends were relentless, however, and finally convinced me to climb up the tower to just look from the 10-foot level. I slowly climbed the ladder and gingerly made my way to the edge to take a peak at the water below. Without hesitation, I turned around and climbed back to safety, where I dove off the *safe* diving board once again. Nevertheless, my friends did not let up. They continued jumping off the platform, while at the same time, assuring me that if I would just trust them to take the leap, I would have much more fun.

A few minutes later they had me up at the 10-foot platform again. This time I continued standing at the edge, trying to gain the courage to jump. But I just knew that if I did jump, I would never make it to the water. My heart nearly pounded out of my chest as I contemplated my fate. I counted "one, two, three," several times, but still could not jump. And then, as in a daze, I stuck my foot out into thin air and pushed off.

For a split second I thought I was going to die. Fear had flooded every muscle in my body, and like a cartoon character, I tried to run in mid-air back to the platform to safety. The attempt was futile. I dropped for what seemed an eternity, leaving my heart back on the ledge. I finally hit the water, submerged, and popped up with the thought, *I'm alive! I'm alive!* My revelation suddenly turned to exhilaration as I *hooped and hollered* all of the way back up to the 10-foot platform, where I leaped without a second thought.

I never had so much fun as jumping off of that scary 10-foot platform, but by that time, my friends had already advanced to the 20-foot platform. I was perfectly content to remain at the level of excitement I had just attained, even though my friends looked like they were having much more fun. I jumped off the 10-foot platform about ten more times until it felt just like jumping off of the 3-foot diving board. It was easy, and now, kind of boring.

It was not too long before my friends talked me into climbing up to the 20-foot platform, and as before, I looked over the edge and immediately climbed back down to the 10-foot level, once again thinking I would surely die if I jumped from 20 feet. I tried a new tactic, attempting to convince my friends that ten feet was plenty high enough, and that they should come down to join me. They would have none of that because they had already tasted the thrill of the higher level.

I finally climbed back up, peered over the edge, and counted, "one, two, three," but could not find the faith to leap. I just knew that I would be the first to die at Surprise Lake. I stood there for 20 minutes, and finally, put my foot out into thin air and pushed off. Once again, I tried to go back, but it was useless. Before I knew it, I was coming up out of the water with the same thought as the first time off of the 10-foot tower: *I'm alive! I'm alive!*

It was not long before my friends were up to the 30-foot tower, and I soon was compelled to join them. I went through the same routine as on the first two levels, and eventually enjoyed the thrill of conquering the *Mount Everest* of diving platforms—for a ten-year-old kid, that is. By the end of the day I felt like a pro as I looked down toward the

3-foot diving board where all of the intimidated kids played.

This story from my childhood illustrates the journey each one of us must take in order to become Ultimate Treasure Hunters. Unfortunately, too many Christians are content to stay where it is safe, staying within the confines of the church where there is little requirement for risk. They look out and can even see the Treasure, but the fear of rejection or failure prevents them from jumping into the adventure God has prepared for them.

Most of us need those who are at the next levels of faith to spur us on toward becoming the Ultimate Treasure Hunter that God intended for us to be. Just like I needed my friends to challenge me to conquer my fears and take the leap of faith, so too, those who have broken through their constraints to go out are needed to call those who are stuck at the safe levels of Christian experience and responsibility to follow. It is when we watch those who have succeeded that we find the supernatural measures of faith within ourselves to attempt the seemingly impossible and dangerous.

A LUMP OF FAITH

We must learn to use the equipment of supernatural faith if we are going to fulfill the Great Commission of making disciples of all of the nations (see Matt. 28:19). The Kingdom of God operates by faith. When the disciples inquired as to why they could not cast the demon out of the boy in Matthew 17:20, Jesus' reply was to the point: "Because you have so little faith. I tell you the truth, if you have faith as small as a mustard seed, you can say to this mountain, 'Move from here to there' and it will move. Nothing will be impossible for you."

God honors faith. In Matthew chapter 9, some blind men approached Jesus. His first response was not to lay hands on them to heal them, but to ask a question in order to test their faith level: "Do you believe that I am able to do this?" When they answered in the affirmative, we are told that He touched their eyes and said, "According to your faith will it be done to you" (Matt. 9:28-29).

In both of the passages above, Jesus never describes the amount of faith required to do miracles. In Matthew chapter 17, you could have the smallest amount of faith and still move mountains. In Matthew chapter 9, Jesus did not put a quantity requirement on their faith level, but was simply looking for a *yes* or *no* to the question.

Hebrews 11:6 informs us that "without faith it is impossible to please God." Again, notice that the writer does not give us an amount of faith required to have faith. No, faith is faith, and unbelief is unbelief. Like yeast (leaven) in bread, just a little will spread throughout the whole lump of dough. So it is with faith and unbelief. If there is even a little of it in our hearts, it will affect every part of us. Therefore, it is not the quantity in question but the quality of our belief in God's promises and His ability to do what He has said is possible.

I love the story of Mary in Luke chapter 1. The angel had told her that she was going to be impregnated by the Holy Spirit and give birth to the Son of God. She obviously did not understand how the Lord was going to accomplish all of this, but her response was one of faith as evidenced in verse 38: "I am the Lord's servant...May it be to me as you have said" (Luke 1:38). And then, in the next scene, Elizabeth greets Mary with these words of affirmation: "Blessed is she who has believed that what the Lord has said to her will be accomplished" (Luke 1:45).

God has called us to be Ultimate Treasure Hunters. He has authorized us as Christ's ambassadors and filled us with the Holy Spirit to be His witnesses. He is looking for those who, like Mary, will respond as the Lord's servants, believing that what the Lord has commissioned us for will be accomplished. He is looking for someone to go to the next level and take a leap of faith, even though the mission seems impossible and dangerous enough that we could die in the process (or at least lose our dignity or convenience). He is looking for one little lump of faith that can be used as a catalyst to launch us into our destiny as Ultimate Treasure Hunters.

JUST DO IT

James tells us "Faith without deeds is dead" (James 2:26). Faith is not only going up to the 10-foot platform, but also stepping out into thin air. Faith leaves no other options. Faith is action. At some point we have to take a leap of faith to do the impossible that God has called us to accomplish. James earlier says:

> *What good is it, my brothers, if a man claims to have faith but has no deeds? Can such faith save him?... faith by itself, if it is not accompanied by action, is dead...Show me your faith without deeds, and I will show you my faith by what I do* (James 2:14-18).

I love the old Nike slogan, "Just Do It," because it summarizes what James was imploring the early Christians to do: to demonstrate their faith expressed in action. At some point, we have to take a leap of faith and pray for someone in a wheelchair if we are going to see breakthrough. We have to be willing to demonstrate the Kingdom inside of us if we want to change the atmosphere around us. We must just do it.

GIFT OF FAITH

Most of the time, when contemplating a new level of risk, a supernatural, supercharged level of faith is needed to take the leap. In First Corinthians 12:9, Paul says that the Spirit gives us faith; we are given a gift of faith. In other words, we are given something we did not have prior to receiving the gift. It is not something we can work up, but it is certainly a gift we can ask for and pursue.

I was leading a Treasure Hunt in Southern California and was directed to a strip mall where we had several clues. One of the clues on my Map was "knee." We found several of the many clues over about a half-hour period and were about ready to leave the site, when I noticed a couple, clearly gang members, walking toward us about 30 yards away. He was walking with a limp, and without a thought, I called out, "Hey, do you by any chance have a hurt knee?"

As we continued to walk closer, it was obvious that this guy did not want to be bothered, but he just sort of stared me down as I drew closer to find the answer to my question. Feeling a little intimidated, I repeated the question, and he responded, "Yeah, what about it?"

I explained the Treasure Hunt and that God had highlighted him to me because He wanted to heal his knee. He countered by saying that he was in a hurry, to which I said that it would not take a long time to fix his knee. "How long would it take?" he asked. Before I could think it through, I boldly proclaimed, "Only a couple of minutes!"

Have you ever wanted to lasso your words and put them back in storage where they belong? Before I could do so, he said "OK, do it." I was past the point of no return. So, another woman who was Treasure Hunting with us (who also had "knee" on her list) and I began to pray. Immediately, his knee was completely healed right there on the sidewalk of the strip mall, and we ended up being able to pray for this couple. When we eventually left, it was as though we were long-time friends.

That was a demonstration of the gift of faith. A boldness and confidence came over me to pronounce somebody being healed—a person and situation I would have normally approached with extreme caution. A gift of faith came on me in this situation to release a "grace" that was appropriate for the situation, and this gang member got healed. I have had many other encounters where a supernatural gift of faith was given to me at just the right moment to do the impossible. Sometimes I have asked for the gift, and other times, like at the strip mall, the Holy Spirit supplied me with the faith needed for an amazing encounter.

MEASURE OF FAITH

Most of the success in Treasure Hunts has come through growing in "measures of faith." In Romans 12:3-8,

Paul describes the "*measure of faith*" God has given each one, as well as operating in gifting in "*proportion to his faith.*" While the "gift of faith" comes on us through supernatural grace, the measure of faith we have seems to be generated within us. The gift of faith is generated in the moment for a specific task or encounter, while the "measure of faith" is the fuel to operate the gift you are employing.

Over the years, I have found that I can grow in the measure of faith in which I operate. In Luke 17:5, the disciples responded to Jesus' command to forgive 70 x 7 times by saying, "increase our faith." Obviously, the disciples did not believe they had it within them to believe for something so seemingly impossible. Furthermore, it was not as though they did not have a measure of faith, but that the measure of faith they had was inadequate for the task at hand. They did not pray, "Give us faith," but "Increase our faith," which meant they needed more of what they already had.

These days, I find myself walking in a much greater measure of faith than when I first started doing Treasure Hunts several years ago. Through the years, I have learned a few principles that have helped me in developing supernatural measures of faith. I continue to explore ways of growing in faith, and hopefully, the principles outlined below will help you in exploring ways of increasing your faith level.

TESTIMONIES

Recently, I was activating a church in New Mexico to get to new levels of breakthrough for physical healing. In one of the ministry times I happened to share the testimony of a time at our church in which Randy Clark was doing a healing conference. He had asked for people to share words of knowledge highlighting those God wanted to touch. God is obviously interested in healing everyone at any time, but utilizing the gift of *word of knowledge* often releases a supernatural gift of faith to believe in the moment for their healing.

Now I had injured my right rotator cuff playing basketball nine months prior, and I had received prayer from several people over that time period, hoping for breakthrough. Those at the conference began shouting out various words of knowledge, which included ailments like *left* rotator cuff, right side of the neck, right bicep, right triceps, but nothing about *right* rotator cuff.

After a few more minutes of other ailments being called out, I became frustrated that I had not heard my specific ailment, which had kept me from some of the activities that I had been able to enjoy before the injury. So, I stood up and called out, "Right rotator cuff!" Yes, I called out my own word of knowledge, and I was instantly healed without anyone praying for me. Interestingly, out of 700 people at the conference, not one other person responded to that word of knowledge.

So, I was sharing this testimony at the church in New Mexico, when a young man jumped out of the crowd that was gathered at the front of the church, and said, "That's me. I'll take that for myself." He began to wildly swing his right arm in a windmill motion, and then sped up until it seemed humanly impossible for his arm to go any faster.

He finally stopped, and with his eyes seemingly five times wider than normal, he yelled out, "I am healed! I am healed!" He then swung his arm around several more times, demonstrating his newfound mobility. He proceeded to tell the congregation that he had been scheduled for surgery the very next week, but now he would call to cancel it because he had been completely healed.

That is the power of the testimony. I keep a Treasure Chest in my office full of the testimonies I have collected over the years. I often use them to fuel my faith to supernatural levels. When my faith level is low, I will often open my Treasure Chest and scan over the many testimonies of breakthrough that occurred as a result of taking risk to leap into my God-given destiny to release the supernatural Kingdom of God in healing or the prophetic.

As I look over what God has done in the past through my leaps of faith, I get encouraged to *do it again* as I feel supernatural measures of faith pouring into my spirit. Similarly, there have been many occasions when I have been on a Treasure Hunt and have been discouraged because we have not found any of the clues on our Treasure Map. As I sense my faith level dropping, I will remind myself (the testimony) of all the times in which I found the clues as I pressed into taking more risk. (I will discuss this point in more detail in the next chapter.)

GIVING AWAY WHAT YOU HAVE

I used to feel very inadequate in my ability to demonstrate the supernatural ministry of the Kingdom of God. I did not feel I was *gifted*, and therefore, had no faith to take the leap to pray for healing or to prophesy, especially in public with people I did not know. I was waiting for God to give me something I did not possess, when all along, He was asking me to give away what I already had.

The problem was that I did not think I had enough. I had the same problem as the disciples in Matthew chapter 14. When they were asked to feed the multitudes of people, they responded that they did not have enough to accomplish the mission. Jesus, on the other hand, gave thanks for what He did have, and then ordered the disciples to give what they had, which led to supernatural increase that left everyone satisfied.

One of my key core values is that when I pray, He comes, and when He comes, He does good things because He is a good God in a good mood. Often, I do not see the immediate effects of the Kingdom being released in people as I pray or prophesy over them until I get a testimony through a letter, phone call, or E-mail. Therefore, I have to continue to operate in faith, knowing that when I pray, good things are happening, despite what I may not be aware of at the moment.

In Luke chapter 6, Jesus says, "Give, and it will be given to you. A good measure, pressed down, shaken together and running over, will be poured into your lap. For with the measure you use, it will be measured to you" (Luke 6:38). So then, when we give out of the resources we have, He gives us back out of the resources He has in His storehouse. Hence, I have learned to give away the measure of faith I have attained, knowing that as I do, He *super-sizes* the *measure* of my faith according to the supernatural measures of the Kingdom.

A few years ago, I had a vision that helped me understand the principle of giving in Luke chapter 6. In the vision, I was standing next to a well in a field. As I looked further, I noticed other wells. Some were capped off, and I could tell that some of the wells had not been accessed for a long while because of the tall, unkempt grass growing up around them.

As I stood in the field gazing over these various wells, I instinctively knew that they contained various resources of the Kingdom of God. For example, the water in one of the wells contained healing, while the water in other wells had love, or the prophetic, wisdom, counsel, joy, and on and on it went. I happened to be standing next to the well containing healing, but I only had a small thimble-sized container in which to dip out of the resources. So, I dipped with what I had available.

As I began to drink of what I had recovered from the well, the Lord told me to pour it out (actually, to toss it out). "But Lord, I won't have any left for me," I responded. Silence. Finally, I got up the nerve to throw out the small measure I had received, heaving it as far as I could. To my surprise, a crop of fruit immediately sprang up in the exact spot where I had thrown the water.

I turned back toward the well, and as I began to dip again, to my amazement, my thimble-sized container had increased to a shot glass-sized container. Once again, I dipped the container into the well and pulled up the water. As before, the Lord said to pour it out. Without hesitation, I threw it in a different direction, and a larger crop of fruit immediately grew where the water had landed.

I went back to the well. This time, my shot-glass container turned into a mug-sized container. I repeated the process again and again until my thimble-sized container had eventually turned into a super-sized, supernatural water truck! The more I gave, the larger my container became, as well as the size of the crops of fruit, as I continued to just give away the new measure I had received.

I then proceeded to the other wells, where I was given a thimble-sized container from which to dip. I went to wells that I had previously drunk from but had quit because of a lack of fruitfulness. I found that as I re-opened those wells and gave away what I had received instead of consuming it myself, supernatural measures were obtained from each of the wells and supernatural fruit was harvested everywhere I had poured out (leaked) the water.

I want to encourage you that you have all of the resources you need to get started on your journey in becoming the Ultimate Treasure Hunter. You can grow in supernatural measures of faith if you continually utilize the testimony and give away what you currently possess, even if it seems thimble-sized. Happy Treasure Hunting!

CHAPTER 10

If at First You Don't Succeed...

‭⁂‬

THE GREATEST TREASURE DISCOVERIES often occur after many seemingly dead-end clues and failed attempts. The best Treasure Hunters are those who do not give up and who continue to take risk until they have found the Ultimate Treasure. There have been many times when we could not find the clues on our Treasure Map, or when we did, the person did not want to give us the time of day. In those times I have felt like I was on an Adventure of Futility instead of the Ultimate Treasure Hunt.

During those times of discouragement I must adjust my attitude to a higher altitude in order to find the motivation to continue looking for the Ultimate Treasure. As I have grown in *measures of faith*, giving away what I have and focusing on past personal testimonies, I have developed an inner confidence that as I persist, I will eventually find the Ultimate Treasure. I have learned that God does not have Treasures hidden *from* me, but *for* me. Therefore, I know that if I keep asking, knocking, and seeking, I will find the hidden Treasure (like the lost coin in Luke 15:9).

REVIVAL AT THE MINI-MART

Several years ago, I was with a pastor out on a Treasure Hunt. He was very excited to see how it worked because while he had a desire to see evangelism in the Church, he was also discouraged with the methods of arguing that he had been accustomed to seeing Christians utilize in their witnessing efforts.

As usual, in our initial Treasure Hunt training, we took about three minutes to get our Treasure Map, and then proceeded to go find the clues. We had an assortment of clues, including "left ankle," "Charles," and "neck pain." Some of our clues led us to an outdoor flea market where I began to ask just about every male if his name was "Charles" as we looked for someone with a potential "left ankle" or "neck" problem.

Oddly enough, among the hundreds of people at the flea market, there was not one person named "Charles," or anyone with physical ailments we had written down as clues. After an hour and a half, we finally gave up.

All the way back to the church I felt embarrassed and repeatedly apologized to the leader, explaining that this was the first time I had been shut out on a Treasure Hunt. He was very gracious, but I could tell that he was disappointed that we had not found one of our clues.

When we got back to the meeting place for all of the teams to share testimonies of the amazing encounters in which Treasures were uncovered, I felt even more embarrassed when I had to share that we came up empty. It almost felt like I was making excuses as I encouraged the group to keep their Treasure Maps available throughout the day, as they may just find more clues later. Once again I apologized to this pastor and encouraged him to continue looking for the clues on his Map, as I would mine.

Some of the group joined me at the mini-mart next door to grab a sandwich at the deli within the store. As we stood there waiting to order our sandwiches, I felt a tap on my shoulder. I turned to find a woman who had been at the healing service I had led the night before. She happily testified that her shoulder, hip, and knee were healed in the meeting.

She also pointed out that the only thing that did not get healed the night before was her "left ankle." I immediately took out my Treasure Map and showed her that "left ankle" was one of the clues I had been looking for on the Treasure Hunt we had just finished. We both became excited at the thought that this was a supernatural, divine encounter. She explained that there were two rods bolting her ankle to the foot, and as a result, she had constant pain and could not move her foot up and down.

Full of supernatural faith, I knelt down and prayed for her, releasing the presence of God on her ankle. Soon, she began to move her foot up and down, and began to run up and down the aisle shouting out, "I'm healed! I'm healed!" She then came back to demonstrate her newfound mobility to her friend who had come into the mini-mart with her.

As we stood together in the aisle marveling at the goodness of God over the miracle we had just witnessed, I introduced myself to her friend, who told me his name was

Dennis. After conversing for several minutes, he handed me his business card. Looking at the card, I saw that his middle name was Dennis, but his first name was "Charles."

Once again, I excitedly pulled out my Treasure Map to show him that, like his friend, he was on it. In addition, he had "neck pain." As we were discussing the odds of these clues being found at just the right time at the mini-mart, a ten-year-old boy came up to us with a Treasure Map. He looked "Charles" up and down, announcing that he had "blue shirt," "blue jeans," and "cowboy boots," which of course "Charles" was wearing.

It just so happened that, like me, this boy had not been able to find any of his clues during the Treasure Hunt. My admonition to continue looking for the clues had encouraged him to keep his Treasure Map. The young boy went on to inquire about some of the other clues he had on his Map. He had "nice guy" and "lousy reader;" Charles confirmed the accuracy of both clues.

He continued with "telephone," "Hawaii," and "headache," at which time Charles' mouth just about dropped to the floor. He explained that just a few minutes before coming into the mini-mart, he had been on the phone with his friend in Hawaii, but had to cut the conversation short because his friend had a severe headache!

There was no doubt; Charles was the Treasure that God was highlighting. We prayed for his neck, which was instantly healed, and then revival broke out in the mini-mart. The joy of the Lord consumed us as we continued ordering our sandwiches. The deli workers began to laugh with us as we shared the testimonies of the two miracles.

We began to prophesy to them, and when we finally left with our sandwiches, everyone in the mini-mart had experienced a demonstration of the goodness and kindness of God.

I learned a great lesson that day: When at first you don't succeed, keep looking, because there are hidden Treasures in some of the least likely places at times when we least expect them. Since this amazing encounter, I have learned to keep my Treasure Map for a period of time after the official Treasure Hunt. Many of the seemingly worthless clues have been found later in the day after all of the other Treasure Hunters have gone home.

JENNIFER

I have also learned that persistence pays off while one is searching for a hidden Treasure. I was on a Treasure Hunt with my daughter, Alexa, and the senior pastor of the church hosting our weekend *Firestorm* conference. I usually like to take the senior pastor out on the Treasure Hunt because if the senior pastor has a good experience, then Treasure Hunting is more likely to become a natural part of the church life.

Alexa had the name "Jennifer" on her map. We also had clues like "plaid green flannel shirt," "birthday," and "cold." Our other clues led us to a crowded downtown area, and I began to ask every female I saw whether her name was "Jennifer." Each time, I was met with a resounding "No," but I persisted, because I knew that if I did not quit, I would eventually find the Treasure I was looking for.

On previous Treasure Hunts, I had found many hidden Treasures through persistence, which had taught me to use the measure of faith that I had already attained. So, because I had faith that I would find "Jennifer," I kept searching. Just as important was my wish to demonstrate the effectiveness of the Treasure Hunt to the pastor who was with us. So, I kept on: "Is your name 'Jennifer'?" and each time I was rejected.

After a little over an hour of many "No's," I decided enough was enough. I told the pastor and my daughter that I was done, that I was not going to ask one more person if her name was "Jennifer." Besides, it was time to go back to the church. So, we headed back to where we had parked, discouraged that we had not had an encounter, other than a few brief casual conversations that did not seem to amount to much.

As we walked down the street, Alexa, who had not taken any risk during the entire Treasure Hunt, casually asked a young woman if her name was "Jennifer." The young woman's boyfriend jumped back, pulling her with him, and yelled, "Who are you? Are you with the police? How did you know her name?"

As startled as the couple, I explained that we were on a Treasure Hunt, and that God had obviously highlighted "Jennifer." Alexa went through the other clues, and we learned that "Jennifer" had a "cold," a "plaid green shirt" hidden under her jacket, and it was her "birthday." After showing them the Treasure Map, they realized that God was truly attempting to get their attention.

"Jennifer" went on to explain that just a few minutes prior to meeting us, she had been approached by someone from our prophetic arts team who had told her that God had impressed upon her to give "Jennifer" a picture she had painted of a rose. She wanted her to know that God really cared about her. As they left, "Jennifer" and her boyfriend marveled at the coincidence of that happening on her "birthday."

So, when Alexa, on her first attempt at a clue that day, asked this young woman if her name was "Jennifer," it had a lot more meaning than we could have known at the time. We found out that "Jennifer" had stopped going to church six years prior, and that her boyfriend had never gone to church. Alexa was able to lead both of them in a prayer to dedicate their lives to Christ, and the pastor gave them information so that they could get involved with the church.

I had given up, but my 12-year-old daughter picked up where my discouragement had ended. Her willingness to step out and take risk where I had not succeeded opened up the possibility to find hidden Treasures. Just think, one more "Is your name 'Jennifer'?" was the tipping point for an amazing divine encounter.

I heard a story of a man who had been digging for gold in the side of a mountain for several years. He had finally given up and had gone to another location, where he also struck out. After years of failure, he decided to go back to the original place where he had thought there may be gold. He made one more swing of the ax and uncovered one of the largest gold veins in California at that time. I want to encourage you that it is often just one more act of risk that uncovers the hidden Treasures around us that are just waiting to be discovered.

THE LAST-MINUTE ENCOUNTER

Recently, I was in Santa Maria doing a *Firestorm* weekend, and as usual, on Saturday morning we trained and sent the church on a Treasure Hunt. Once again, I was with the pastor of the church, accompanied by his son, and Chad, my son. We were having a great time all together doing the *father-son* Treasure Hunt, as we went from encounter to encounter.

I knew in my spirit, however, that even though we had already had a few really good encounters, an amazing encounter was still waiting for us. We finally made our way to "Wal-Mart," which was next to a "stop sign," next to a "bench," next to a large outdoor "fountain," all clues found on each of our four maps. I also had "Sandra" on my map, so I waited for "Sandra."

A few minutes went by, as I got up the courage to ask if anyone was named "Sandra." About this time, another Treasure Hunting group came by, and we shared some brief testimonies of what had happened previously. I shared that while we had already had some good encounters, I had been looking for an extreme over-the-top encounter.

I noticed that it was time to return to the church to share testimonies, but I felt like I just could not leave the "fountain" without at least attempting to find a "Sandra." I said to the other Treasure Hunter, "I only have one minute left, and I have to find 'Sandra.'" When I turned to scan the area around the fountain, I noticed a woman pushing a stroller.

Knowing that I did not have any time to waste at this point, I asked, "Excuse me, but by any chance is your name 'Sandra'?" She responded, "Why, do I have a name badge on?" She did not have a name badge on, and I proceeded to tell her about the Treasure Hunt.

She started crying and explained that she had been at the hospital where her 80-year-old father was dying. She had been at the hospital all night long and throughout the entire morning, and had just told her family that she needed to go for a walk to get some perspective on the imminent death of her father.

I began to prophesy how the Father had highlighted her because He wanted her to know how much He cared for her, and that He was with her in her moment of need to comfort and strengthen her. I went on to tell her that I had been looking for her since the beginning of the Treasure Hunt, and that our time had almost run out when I had found her. She repeatedly thanked me for stopping her and said that she was going back to the hospital to tell her entire family about the amazing encounter she had just experienced.

This is just one more example of continuing to look for the Ultimate Treasure until it is found. In the parable of Luke chapter 15, the woman searched and searched until she found the lost coin. We are not told, but the implication is that she checked many places without finding the coin she was looking for. How many times do we give up because we have not had immediate success? Ultimate Treasure Hunters are those who employ patience and persistence in finding the Ultimate Treasure.

WHO OWNS THE WHITE HONDA CIVIC?

Sometimes, we do not find the encounters at the clues we are led to, but they lead us to other clues that lead us to divine encounters. On a Treasure Hunt, it is important to follow the clues, wherever they may lead, and persist in looking for hidden Treasure, even when it seems like you have not succeeded.

Each week, during our outreach time at the School of Supernatural Ministry, I oversee about 25 teams of Treasure Hunters going out into the city of Redding, California. Each week, these 100 students come back with amazing stories of incredible encounters in which people get saved, healed, and delivered. Most of the encounters occur as the students find their clues on the Treasure Map, then get prophetic words for the people they find. Many of these encounters occur after it appears that a team has been led to a seemingly futile clue.

Recently, Rebecca, one of our second-year Treasure Hunt student leaders shared a testimony about the encounters her group had while on an hour-and-a-half Treasure Hunt.

She writes:

My Group had a series of clues, including "stoplight," "Cypress," "parking lot," and "Starbucks." So we drove down Churn Creek Road until the stoplight that intersects this road with "Cypress." To our left was a "Starbucks" and a huge "parking lot." So we decided to check out the location for any further clues.

As we pulled into the parking lot, Chris mentioned that he had a "white car" on his Treasure Map, to which I responded that I had a "white Honda Civic" as a clue. When we pulled around to the *Starbucks* coffee shop, we immediately noticed a *white Honda Civic*! We were so encouraged by the obvious clue that we waited there to tell the owner that he or she was the Treasure on our list. After several minutes, the owner had not shown up, so I asked my team tentatively, "What should we do now?" to which came the response, "I don't know, you're the leader!"

Since Chris also had "chicken" on his list, I decided to head to the supermarket across the "parking lot." Standing outside smoking a cigarette was a young lady with her male friend. She was dressed all in black, with a burgundy apron, which matched the description that team member Kawika had on his appearance list: "all black" and "burgundy."

We approached the young lady and showed her the clues on our list that had brought us to her. She became freaked out and asked us what we wanted from her! We told her that God had highlighted her and wanted to bless her. She responded that God wouldn't do that for her.

We continued in conversation and found that they both did not think that they were worth our prayers, that there were so many more people who needed them, that they were not worthy of God's attention. They began to share about the tragic things that had happened to the people around them. Then the lady, Annie, had to go back to work.

I followed her and asked if I could walk with her because there was something that I wanted to tell her. I really did not know what I was going to tell her at the time, but I knew God wanted to touch her, so I got a prophetic word as we walked.

I began telling her that I saw a gift of counsel on her and that her heart was growing toward the justice and social work system, as I noted that she had a heart for children most of all. I asked if she had children, which she did, and if there was a hard situation with them right now. She nodded and her hands began to shake as she began to tear up. I asked if the court was involved, and she began to cry. She was going through a divorce and a custody battle. (I found out later that Kawika had "divorce" on his Treasure Map.)

After those prophetic insights, I was able to pray with her and let her know that God was interested in her situation, that He cared, and that He had a plan to work out her situation for good. She hugged me, thanked me profusely, and continued on back to work. As she left, she expressed how excited she was that God knew and cared about her.

Meanwhile, Chris began sharing with the girl's friend. Chris had a *word of knowledge* about a dream the man had the night before. He responded that he had had a dream, and in it someone had come to talk to him about Jesus, just as Chris was doing! Chris also received another word of knowledge about him being a seer and having seen angels since he was little.

The young man freaked out!! He could not believe that God would tell someone this secret stuff about him! It turned out that the young man had attended Bethel Christian school when he was young and had received Jesus into his heart, but hadn't been following God. That day, however, he found out that God was following him instead!

After another encounter, we finally left the store and came across someone I knew, who happened to have an injury to his left leg for which we prayed. After praying, he told us that he had never experienced so much of God's presence, especially in front of a supermarket!

We headed back toward the "white Honda Civic," but there was still no one there. While walking, we spotted a homeless man in a wheelchair, who seemed like a good target! We bought him a meal, and I asked him if he had "heart problems" because that was on my list! He did, and also "knee problems," which was on another list.

We prayed and released the kingdom into his body. While he said he didn't feel any different after he had checked himself out, there was a noted difference in his countenance. Chris had a word of knowledge that he used to do construction, at which the homeless man began to laugh because he did! We then prophesied longevity and a new release of life. He expressed how touched he was that God knew about him and even bothered to tell three random young people!

These students never did find the owner of the "white Honda Civic," but because they did not stop at their seeming lack of success, they found hidden Treasures all around them. The point is this: If at first you don't succeed, don't stop, keep going, and take another swing. If these students had stopped at the "white Honda Civic," they may never have had the amazing encounters God had set up for them. Likewise, if they had not continued to pursue the "white Honda Civic," they might have missed the divine appointment with the homeless man.

GIVE IT A CHANCE

In addition to persisting in finding clues, I have had many occasions in which I have felt like giving up on a potential Treasure because they do not seem to be responding favorably. Often during these encounters, I will continue to build rapport, asking open-ended questions while looking for an opportunity to demonstrate and/or share the good news.

I often have to remind myself that many of the best encounters I have had came just after I felt like giving up in a conversation. The breakthrough came as a result of one more question, or, stepping out in one more *word of knowledge* or prophetic word. There have been so many times when I have become impatient as I met resistance from a potential Treasure, and as a result, tended to give up too easily.

Often, people just need time to process. In Acts chapter 26, Paul is defending his faith and actions to King Agrippa. He gives a detailed account of his testimony, as well as the good news of the gospel. Afterwards, he asks King Agrippa if he believes the prophets (see Acts 26:27). King Agrippa responds, "Do you think that in such a short time you can persuade me to be a Christian?"

Paul's answer in the next verse is very wise: "Short time or long—I pray God that not only you but all who are listening to me today may become what I am, except for these chains." It seems that Paul was not so concerned with the timing of Agrippa's being saved, but that he would eventually give his life to Christ. He truly believed that his persistence in witnessing would eventually pay off.

As we read on, it seems as though, while King Agrippa did not immediately give his life to Christ, he surely was sympathetic with Paul's mission. In order to be successful at Treasure Hunting, it is imperative that we appreciate the process as much as the discovery of the Treasure. For some, it often takes several divine encounters before they are convinced that God is good and has a good plan for their life.

Once again, we must have the same perspective as God, in that "He is patient with you, not wanting anyone to perish, but everyone to come to repentance" (2 Pet. 3:9). Along with this, we must also keep in mind that it is His kindness that leads people to repentance (see Rom. 2:4). The Treasure Hunt is simply designed to demonstrate the goodness and kindness of God expressed through supernatural measures of faith as we persist to find the gold in each Treasure that God leads us to.

God never gives up on someone. Like the thief on the cross in Luke chapter 23:42-43, God is always working toward redemptive purposes in someone's life, even up until their last breath. Many would have given up on this man, thinking he had missed his opportunity and was therefore a lost cause, but Jesus was not done with the Treasure Hunt! Our job is to continue persisting even when the outcome does not seem as potentially successful, while God's job is to draw them. As we do our job, He is faithful to do His job. Ultimate Treasure Hunters never give up.

CHAPTER 11

Treasure Hunting Is a Lifestyle, Not an Event

꧁◈꧂

I WAS SHOPPING IN THE LOCAL MALL with my daughter one early evening when we came across Jerry, one of our School of Supernatural Ministry students. He had a frantic look on his face as he informed us that he only needed "one more" before he could go home. Thinking he was after merchandise of some kind, we offered to help. He pulled out a piece of paper and asked if we had seen anyone with a wrist brace.

He went on to explain that he had been working on his Treasure Hunting skills and had decided to train at the mall. He had written down ten words of knowledge and had vowed not to go home to his wife and four children until he had found all ten clues! Jerry is an amazing Treasure Hunter who has learned that Treasure Hunting is supposed to be a continual lifestyle rather than a one-time programmed event.

I have had many reports from churches and individuals who are doing Treasure Hunts as a supernatural lifestyle. Some are meeting once a week to do group Treasure Hunts, while others are sitting for a few minutes each day to prepare a Treasure Map to take with them to work or to school. I even heard of one woman who does a Treasure Hunt each week with her sister who lives 3,000 miles away. They call each other to exchange clues, and then spend a few hours looking for them. Once they are done, they call each other to report what they found.

Each time I take teams from Bethel's School of Supernatural Ministry to do *Firestorms*, I utilize the Treasure Hunt to equip, empower, and activate the churches we are working with into supernatural evangelism through supernatural encounters. Our hope, however, is that they will gain confidence to continue to do supernatural evangelism once we are gone, whether it is utilizing the Treasure Hunt, or some other creative strategy.

The Treasure Hunt is undoubtedly an effective mechanism to mobilize people for supernatural evangelism, but a person does not need to do a Treasure Hunt to do supernatural evangelism. Obviously, any believer can heal the sick, raise the dead, set people free, and lead people to Christ apart from doing a Treasure Hunt.

Treasure Hunting clearly promotes and facilitates tapping into the supernatural resources of the Kingdom to bring Heaven to earth (see Matt. 6:9-10). The point, however, is to demonstrate the Kingdom through our witness in whatever creative ways God directs us, that we live naturally supernatural lives, so that we exude His presence wherever we go.

While the Treasure Map has proven to help us find Treasures we would not have ordinarily considered, we do not necessarily need supernatural *clues* to find hidden Treasure. There are Treasures all around us, and we can find them everywhere as we inconvenience ourselves to "stop for the one," as Heidi Baker has so demonstratively taught and modeled in her ministry to the hundreds of Mozambican orphans she is helping in Africa. Likewise, when our eyes are opened to the hundreds we pass by every day, we cannot help but to be filled with compassion to offer the help that we can supernaturally provide.

IF WE OPEN OUR EYES, HE WILL OPEN THEIR EYES

Recently, while in prayer, my son, Chad, had an encounter in which he heard God say that He was going to teach him how to pray. He was directed to Matthew 6:9-10 and could not get past the phrase, "Our Father, who is in Heaven," reading it over several times.

As he contemplated these verses, he heard God ask him to describe what came to mind when he heard the phrase "Our Father." My son's reply was, "Your children, the Church," but God responded, "That's not big enough; you have to think bigger. You have to think about your city and the world." He went on to say that He was going to give him a sign that day, and that He was going to teach him that when he took ownership for the unsaved of the world in his prayers, it would release the greatest wave of evangelism the world has ever seen.

After praying, he went about his day looking for the sign. Nothing seemed to stand out as the sign until that afternoon when he saw a woman wearing a knee brace, driving a motorized cart in the grocery store. He approached the woman to inquire about the apparent injury and found out that she had recently fallen off some stairs and torn the ligaments in her knee. She continued to explain that she also had severe neck pain from the accident.

He eventually asked the woman if she would allow him to pray for her. She informed him that she was Hindu and did not believe in his God, but that he could go ahead and pray. So, right there in the middle of aisle 12 of a local supermarket, he laid his hand on her shoulder and released the presence of Christ.

After a short prayer, she reported that she felt fire in her back, and immediately all of the pain left. He then asked about her knee. She responded that she could not tell what was happening without taking off the knee brace. He instructed her to take it off, and after doing so, she began walking up and down the aisle without any pain or limp.

She then told him that she wanted the same Jesus he had and received Jesus in her heart. Soon after, as he was standing in line to pay for his groceries, he heard an announcement over the intercom instructing one of the employees to retrieve the abandoned motorized cart in aisle 12! Marveling at the miraculous sign that had just occurred, he heard the Lord say, "That is not the sign."

A little confused, he made his way back to the car. En route, he noticed a man with a patch covering his right eye. Instantly, the Lord spoke to him and said, "This is the sign I am giving you today." Chad stopped the man to ask him why he had a patch over his eye and found out that he was completely blind. As Chad placed his hand over the patched eye, the man felt an immediate change. He then removed the patch to discover that his blind eye had been completely healed.

At that moment, the Lord spoke to my son and said, "This is what I will do if the Church will be the light and take ownership of the world: I will open up the eyes of the unsaved." In other words, if we will open our eyes, then He will open their eyes.

In Second Corinthians 4:4, Paul points out that, "The god of this age has blinded the minds of unbelievers, so that they cannot see the light of the gospel of the glory of Christ, who is the image of God." The sign Chad received was not so much about healing someone's eye, as it was about enabling someone to see Christ by removing the spiritual blindness. Certainly, the healing of this man's blind eye was amazing, but miracles themselves are signs pointing to Christ. God wants to heal eyes, but He ultimately wants to open people's spiritual eyes to see the Kingdom.

In Luke 10:17-19, the disciples were excited about the amazing miraculous breakthroughs they had experienced, while Jesus' focus was on the eternal consequences: "Rejoice because your names are written in Heaven." The ultimate goal for any supernatural encounter is to establish or increase relationship with God. The question is whether or not we will be willing to open our eyes to the *blind* around us; will we take ownership for the world that God has placed in our sphere of influence?

LIGHT OF THE WORLD ON THE CHAIR LIFT

Last ski season I was paired up with a 30-year-old man to ride on the chair lift at a local ski area. On the way up to the top of the mountain, I noticed that he was wincing in apparent pain. He explained that a few days prior he had been bitten by a brown recluse spider two times, once on the left side of his chest, and the other on the back of his left shoulder. The bites had caused the muscles on the left side of his body to be somewhat paralyzed, while at the same time leaving him riddled with pain.

He had already taken one run down the mountain and found that he could barely ski because of the debilitating effects of the spider's venom. He had planned to go up one more time to see if he could work out the stiffness, but the pain had increased so much from the physical exertion of the first run that he was worried that he might not be able to make it down the mountain the second time.

Realizing the pain he was experiencing, I asked what he had done to treat the symptoms. He told me that his wife had forced him to go to a "light therapist," who focused certain types of ultraviolet light on the infected areas. I asked, "How is that working out for you?" to which he replied, "Not too good!" He went on to explain that this "light therapist" was the only apparent hope he had to treat the pronounced symptoms, but that he had received several treatments without any noticeable change in his condition.

I casually mentioned that I had access to a more powerful light that could take care of his problem. That got his attention, and he asked what kind of light I was speaking of, to which I responded, "It's the Light of the world, Jesus, and He can heal you right here, right now." He explained that he had never believed in Jesus, but agreed to let me pray for him as we were heading up to the top of the mountain on the chair lift.

So, I just simply released the light of the presence of Christ on him in a very short prayer without touching him, and then asked him to tell me what he was experiencing. To my surprise, and his, all of the pain had completely left his body.

He was so excited about the immediate change that he began to ask questions about my belief in Christ. After I quickly answered a few questions, he expressed that he had always thought of Christianity as just another philosophy, not a relationship with a living God. I briefly explained that he could have a relationship with Jesus, and that he could experience His presence any time he wanted, to which he responded that he was already feeling a presence all over him and that this was all very foreign to him.

Knowing I had only a short time before we reached the top of the mountain, I asked how the numbness in his muscles was doing. He stretched a little, and then reported that there was still no change. Hearing the status, I asked if he would like another session of the "Light therapy." He readily agreed.

Once again, I released God's presence in a simple, short prayer, and asked how he felt. With a shocked look on his face, he exclaimed that all of the numbness was gone, "But wait a minute," he said, "let me get off of the chair lift to check it out," as if I had used some kind of spell on him to make him temporarily *think* he was healed.

Nevertheless, it was obvious that he was shaken by the encounter of God's presence surrounding the chair lift, which prompted more questions. I answered a few, and then blessed him as we disembarked from the lift.

I skied over to my wife and daughter, who had been in the chair in front of us, and began to help them with their snowboards. In the midst of our getting everything adjusted, the man skied over to inform me that all of the pain and numbness was gone. He was so excited that he yelled out a big "Thank you," and then skied off down the mountain as though he was in a race!

I'm sure he had a lengthy conversation with his wife that evening about the other "Light Therapist" he had encountered that day! I did not have a Treasure Map with me while skiing that day, but God placed me right next to a Treasure on the chair lift. All it took to find the clue was for me to look at the need, and then take some risk to meet it.

Treasure Hunting is simply living naturally supernaturally wherever we go; it is a supernatural lifestyle. There are clues all around us calling us to divine appointments with lost Treasures. A true Treasure Hunter is simply one who brings Heaven to earth to whoever they meet. Like this example of the man on the chair lift, as we take ownership for the needs around us, God will reveal Himself to those we touch in His name.

ANOINTED BEYOND OUR ABILITY

I suppose many believers are intimidated by ministering in the supernatural because they just do not feel like they have the necessary ability to confidently release the Kingdom. I want to propose, however, that every believer has the potential to operate in the supernatural; every believer has the potential ability to heal the sick, prophesy, and set people free. Unfortunately, too many today are unaware that they are actually anointed beyond their ability.

In John 17:18, as Jesus was praying for the disciples, He said to the Father, "As You sent Me into the world, I have sent them into the world." Similarly, after the resurrection, Jesus informed the disciples in John 20:21 saying, "As the Father has sent Me, I am sending you."

There are two questions that we must ask in order to understand the significance of Jesus' commission to the disciples. The first is "Why was He sent?" and then second, "How was He sent?" The answer to these two questions will give us the insight into why and how we are to be sent.

In order to answer the *why* question, we must look to Jesus' first sermon recorded in Luke 4:18-19. In this inaugural message, Jesus stated, "He has sent Me to proclaim freedom for the prisoners and [He has sent Me to proclaim] recovery of sight for the blind, [He has sent Me] to release the oppressed, [He has sent Me] to proclaim the year of the Lord's favor." Jesus was specifically sent to accomplish these four things, which are in fulfillment of the Messianic mission found in Isaiah 61:1-7.

We are, therefore, *sent* to do the same things Jesus did, "As the Father has **sent Me**, I am **sending you**." We have been *sent* to proclaim freedom for the prisoners, recovery of sight for the blind, to release the oppressed, and to proclaim the year of the Lord's favor. In other words, we are to release the Kingdom wherever we go to whomever we meet. That was His mission, and it is our mission as well.

Next, we need to know *how* Jesus accomplished His mission because from my perspective that mission seems impossible for me to accomplish. For the answer, we must turn back to Jesus' first sermon in Luke chapter 4. In quoting

Isaiah 61:1, Jesus announced that, "The Spirit of the Lord is on Me, because He has anointed Me...." Hence, the way Jesus was able to fulfill the mission His Father had given Him was that the Holy Spirit anointed Him. In other words, He was anointed beyond His ability.

In Acts 10:38, Peter explained that, "God anointed Jesus of Nazareth with the Holy Spirit and power," and that, "He went around doing good and healing all who were under the power of the devil, because God was with Him." Jesus was called to an impossible mission that could only have been accomplished by being anointed with the Holy Spirit. So then, like Jesus, we too must be anointed with the Holy Spirit in order to be anointed beyond our ability.

The word for *anointing* in the Hebrew language is *messhiach*, from which we get the English word *Messiah*, which means "Anointed One." The Greek counterpart to *messhiach* is *christos*, from which we get the English word, Christ. The term *Christian* is the Greek word *christianos*, "anointed ones," and is from the same root as *Christos*, which is *chrio* (to anoint).

Chrio, having the connotation of anointing an *individual* for a specific purpose, is different from the Greek word *aleipho* (the Hebrew, *suk*), which is the *act* of anointing. For example, when Mary anointed (*aleipho*) Jesus' feet with perfume, Mary was not anointed, but the *act* itself brought about the anointing. In James 5:14, we are instructed to anoint (*aleipho*) the sick. In that case, it is the act itself that brings about the healing, not the person doing the act.

Chrio, on the other hand, is anointing *a person* to accomplish a mission or responsibility. For example, the kings in the Old Testament were all anointed (*messhiach*) to defeat the enemies of Israel, as well as to provide and protect the blessings of God for the people. In the same way, the priests were anointed (*messhiach*) to perform specific duties in the Temple, ensuring that the people would continue in right standing before God.

Interestingly, Jesus is described as the royal *"KING OF KINGS"* (Rev. 19:16) and our "great high Priest" (Heb. 4:14). He was the *Messhiach* king and the *Messhiach* priest commissioned to bring the Kingdom to those who would believe. Likewise, in First Peter 2:9, we are described as a "royal priesthood."

So then, just as Jesus was anointed by the Holy Spirit at His baptism, so too, when Jesus breathed on the disciples, the *royal priesthood*, in John 20:22, they were also anointed (*chrio*). In the same way, Christians (*christianos*) today are also anointed as the Holy Spirit is breathed on us, which means that, like Jesus and the disciples, we get anointed beyond our ability.

Saul is a great example of someone who was anointed (*messhiach*) beyond his ability. In First Samuel chapter 10, the prophet Samuel came to anoint (*messhiach*) Saul, whom God had just selected to be king over Israel. Samuel anoints (*messhiach*) Saul with oil in verse 1, and goes on to inform him in verses 6 and 7 that:

> *The Spirit of the Lord will come upon you in power, and you will prophesy with them* [the prophets]*; and you will be changed into a different person. Once these signs are fulfilled, do whatever your hand finds to do, for God is with you.*

The anointing (*messhiach*) enabled Saul to do what he had not been able to do before. He was anointed beyond his ability. As the anointed (*messhiach*) king, he was also granted the authority to govern in the way he saw fit. He could rule with confidence because God with was with him, implying that God was backing up his decisions.

It was the same way for the disciples. Back in John 20:23 notice that Jesus gave them authority to do what they could not have done on their own. Along with the anointing comes the authority to do what they had been commissioned to do. He was basically saying that whatever they decided to do, He would back them up.

Jesus told them, "If you forgive anyone's sins, they are forgiven; if you do not forgive them, they are not forgiven." Only God can forgive sins, which is why the religious leaders accused Jesus of blasphemy in Luke 5:21. Yet Jesus was able to forgive sins because He was anointed, and with that anointing came the authority to do only what God could do.

To forgive sins was to release Kingdom authority, which was the point of Luke 5, that it was just as easy to heal someone, as it was to forgive their sins. Both require authority from God. Similarly, when Jesus announced that the disciples had authority to forgive sins, He was also implying that they had authority to heal the sick, prophesy, and set people free from demonic strongholds. The "if" meant that it was up to the disciples to do it, that like Saul, they had the authority because of their anointing to pursue "whatever their hands found to do."

Jesus was sent with a mission to destroy the works of the devil and usher in the blessings of Heaven. We have been sent with the same mission: "As the Father has sent Me, I am sending you." Jesus could not have done the mission without an impartation of anointing through the Holy Spirit. He used His authority to bring Heaven to earth. So too, when we pray, the Kingdom comes because we have authority through the impartation of anointing (*messhiach/chrio*) we have received.

"WHAT A LAZY PRAY-ER!"

Knowing that I am anointed and authorized to release the Kingdom increases the confidence I have to know that when I pray, something is happening. This confidence has allowed me to live an extraordinary, naturally supernatural lifestyle.

Moreover, in releasing the Kingdom, I have found that I do not have to whip up the anointing with the volume or the number of my words. No, when I pray, the Kingdom comes because I am praying with the authorized right to bring Heaven to earth.

Several months ago at one of our Pastors'/Leaders' Advances, a pastor approached me after the last meeting and asked if I would be willing to pray for him. He explained that he was an avid skier and had, five months prior, sustained a strange injury while skiing. Both of his arches had fallen at the same time, leaving his feet completely flat. This had caused such excruciating pain that he could not continue skiing down the mountain and had to be transported to the medical center in the ski-patrol sled.

The debilitating pain kept him from putting any weight on his feet, so that he could not walk. He was referred to a doctor who made special inserts for his shoes so that he could walk with mild pain, but could still only walk about 50 feet without severe pain. He expressed how desperate he was to be healed, in that the debilitation had completely altered his lifestyle and ministry.

I readily agreed to pray for him, so as we stood among the crowd of people making their way out of the conference, I gently placed my foot over the top of his foot and put my hand on his shoulder. I began sharing testimonies of how I had seen feet healed in the past, how I saw a young girl's flat feet grow arches before my eyes as I outlined imaginary arches on her flat feet with my index finger. All the while, even as I continued to pray, I periodically moved my foot back and forth to each of his feet.

Two months later, he came back to Bethel to confess that he had held judgment toward me for the way I had prayed for him at the Pastors'/Leaders' Advance. He told me that as I was praying, he was thinking, "This is the laziest pray-er I have ever seen. This guy is so lazy that he won't even bend down to pray for my feet. I came here, all the way to Bethel, and this is what I get?" He went on to tell me that after I had prayed that night, he left feeling disappointed and angry that a Bethel pastor would have so little compassion.

As he had walked toward his car after the *lazy* prayer, however, the arches in his feet became so painful that he had to sit down under a tree in the parking lot. He decided to take his shoes off to examine the source of the pain, and when he did, the pain left. He then looked down to find that both of his feet had developed brand-new arches. He removed the supports from his shoes and began to walk with no more pain.

As he shared this testimony, he apologized for his attitude, and thanked me for mine. He came to realize that it is not the way in which we pray that brings about breakthrough, but the authority in which we are praying. Laying feet on people is not the new and improved formula for healing miracles. It is the Kingdom within us, and the Kingdom released through us that provides breakthrough.

Ultimate Treasure Hunters are simply those who understand the anointing they have received through the Holy Spirit, and then utilize the authority they have been entrusted with to destroy the works of the devil and release the blessings of God. Ultimate Treasure Hunters are simply those who live naturally supernatural lifestyles.

CHAPTER 12

Getting the Treasure Into the Treasure Chest

ᴀ✵◎⊛✵ᴢ

O UR TREASURE MAP LED US to a coffee shop where we found someone from our list of clues with a "hurt right shoulder." A team that my wife, Theresa, was leading was already ministering to him, so when we came in and identified him as a highlighted Treasure on our map, he was obviously intrigued about the encounter. After several minutes of conversation, we asked if he would like us to pray for his shoulder. He explained that he was not a Christian and did not believe in this "hocus pocus" stuff.

After we explained that he had nothing to lose and everything to gain, he agreed to let us pray for him. So, as he stood there with a cup of mocha in his hand, we laid our hands on his shoulder and he was instantly healed. He was so overwhelmed that he had actually been healed that he began to ask who we were and what we believed. After several more minutes of conversation, we invited him to the healing service we were holding back at the church where we were doing a *Firestorm* conference.

That night, we invited all who wanted an impartation for more of God's presence to come forward. Several who had been at the coffee shop earlier that day soon noticed that the man who had been healed was now at the front of the church along with his young daughter. Both of them received Christ in their hearts that night and were among the last to leave the building as they had been so touched by God's presence.

MAKING DISCIPLES OF CONVERTS

The goal of the Treasure Hunt is to make disciples of those we find with our clues. In Matthew chapter 28:18-20, Jesus' commission was to make disciples not converts. There have been many who have been in a high-powered service in which they made a decision to go forward to repeat a prayer, but making a decision does not necessarily make a disciple.

In Acts chapter 2, we are told that "The Lord added to their number daily those who were being saved" (Acts 2:47). The purpose of our witness, then, is to get people into the Kingdom, of which the Church is its representative while here on earth (see Eph. 2:21). So in a sense, getting someone into the Kingdom is to get someone into the Church.

At Bethel Church, we love to see people encounter Christ out in the community, but we really get excited when we hear that they have been connected to a local church, whether it is ours or another church in the city. We are interested in the expansion of the Kingdom, not necessarily just our particular church. We do, however, see many get saved through our various outreach ministries and make their way into our church where they can get discipled.

The final objective of the Treasure Hunt is to get the Treasure into the Treasure Chest; it is to get the convert into the Church. In the parable of the lost coin, the implication is that God was not content to leave the "coin" where He had found it, but called all of His friends together to rejoice with Him in what He had found (see Luke 15:8-10). The Treasure Hunt, then, is not over until the "lost coin" is safely stored with the other coins in the Treasure Chest.

An Open Invitation to All

Unfortunately, we do not always have the opportunity to bring someone to church, for a variety of reasons, but it is something we are always instructing as a primary objective of the Treasure Hunter. With this in mind, it is good to bring along a business-type card with service times, contact information, and directions on the back. It is kind of like giving them a wedding invitation. In addition, it is also helpful, when possible, to get their contact information for further follow-up.

In the parable of the wedding banquet in Matthew chapter 22, the directive was to invite everyone to the banquet, but although all were eventually invited, not everyone took advantage of the open invitation. Sadly, people made all kinds of excuses, even though God's intention was to fill the wedding hall with guests.

The Treasure Hunt is going to the "street corners" (the community), and gathering all of the people (Treasures) we can find (see Matt. 22:8-10). It is important to remember, however, that our commission is to invite them, not make them come. Notice that God's focus was on finding the people who would respond, not on those who did not. God was willing to get a lot of "No's" in order to get some "Yes's." His heart is to invite everyone, in hopes that even a few would make their way into the Treasure Chest.

I was on a Treasure Hunt recently in which we were constantly getting "No's" from people who were clearly on our Treasure Maps. We were finally led to a man who, several years prior, had lost both parents to illness and lost his lucrative job of many years; his wife divorced him, after which he lost his home, and he finally ended up on the streets as an alcoholic.

He told us that a few years prior he had gone through a program that had helped him get sober, but he still had no vision for his life. Consequently, he continued roaming aimlessly from town to town, taking odd jobs, just trying to find a break somewhere. The man was "clean-cut" and was obviously sober, but was visibly depressed over his unfortunate circumstances.

Interestingly, we were the last of three other teams that were led to this man. Without realizing it, all three teams went to work independently to try to find this man a place to stay where he could discover and begin to live out his God-given destiny. Giving the man directions, each of the teams had invited him to the *Firestorm* conference that evening. The man showed up, and when I asked if anyone wanted to know the good, kind God that we had been presenting and demonstrating through the prophetic and healing that evening, this man was the first one standing to invite Jesus into his life!

As it turned out later, one of the Treasure Hunt team members worked out an arrangement where the man could live at his house while he got discipled and sorted out his career options. As a result, this man now has an opportunity to enter into the plans and purposes that God has prepared for him, which is the purpose of getting the Treasure into the Treasure Chest!

Although we do not successfully get everyone we meet into the Treasure Chest, our goal is to give him or her more than a one-time encounter. We must always keep in mind that supernatural encounters are signs leading people into an ongoing relationship with God and connection with the family of God, the Church, where they can be nurtured into maturity and given the tools and support to live successfully in the Kingdom.

You Can't Follow Me

Some Christians, however, tend to discount the witnessing process, using the argument that there is not enough follow-up. They contend that it does more harm than good to witness if the proper mechanisms of follow-up are not set up to get people into the Church. Their argument is that Jesus commanded us to make disciples, not converts.

That is true, but although making disciples is the ultimate objective, it is important to keep in mind that before we can disciple them, we must first convert them through a "born-again" encounter. We must not allow ourselves, therefore, to devalue witnessing just because the Church has done a poor job in making disciples.

Jesus preached the gospel wherever He went, healing the sick and setting people free, yet only four people were found at the cross with Him while He was crucified. Out of the more than 500 who saw Him after the resurrection (see 1 Cor. 15:6), only 120 were found in the Upper Room on the Day of Pentecost (see Acts 1:15). The point is that Jesus gave everyone a chance to get in, even if they did not take advantage of the opportunity. Nowhere does Jesus ever heal someone or set someone free with the condition that they follow Him as a disciple.

On the contrary, in the Gospel of Luke, we find a story of a demon-possessed man from the region of the Gerasenes (see Luke 8:26-39). This man had been harassed by a "Legion" of demons, causing him to run around naked, homeless, and chained hand and foot. It seemed only natural for him to want to follow Jesus once he was set free, but we are told that Jesus sent him away even though the man begged Him. Jesus commanded, "Return home and tell how much God has done for you" (Luke 8:39).

Remarkably, in verse 40, when Jesus returned some time later, a crowd welcomed Him, even though back in verse 37 all of the people of that region had previously asked Him to leave. So then, even though this man who had been set free through an encounter with Jesus had not been discipled, he was still able to continue in the revelation he had received, as well as influence the entire region through his testimony.

SOWING SEED

Interestingly, in the parable of the seed and the sower in Matthew chapter 13, only 25 percent of the seed actually produced fruit. The seed, however, was sown equally into each type of soil without discrimination. Obviously, it is God's heart that all of the seed He sows becomes fruitful, but the fact that it does not, does not prevent Him from sowing. Like Christ, we have to trust that the seed of the message of the Kingdom (see Matt. 13:19) will find a receptive heart that will cultivate what has been sown.

The apostle Paul points out in First Corinthians 3:6 that, "I planted the seed, Apollos watered it, but God made it grow." While our goal is to see people established into the Kingdom, our job is to do our job, whatever task may be required in the process. Sometimes Paul planted, while at other times he watered what someone else had planted. Regardless, God's job was to always bring the growth to the seed.

A good example of this principle was when Philip was supernaturally led by the Holy Spirit to meet the Ethiopian eunuch in Acts chapter 8. This was an amazing Treasure Hunt in which the eunuch was miraculously saved as Philip obeyed the Holy Spirit's guidance. And then, interestingly, as Philip baptized him, we are told that, "When they came up out of the water, the Spirit of the Lord suddenly took Philip away, and the eunuch did not see him again, but went on his way rejoicing" (Acts 8:39).

Wait a minute. He did not have time to get him into a local church. What was the Holy Spirit thinking? Why did He not allow Philip to stay with him long enough to get "added" to the church? Could it be that God trusted that what had been sown would produce the fruit that was intended? Church historical accounts from early Apostolic Fathers of the Faith such as Irenaeus (a.d. 130–202) indicate that this eunuch went back to Ethiopia and was very influential in establishing the gospel in Ethiopia as well as other parts of northern Africa.

We are often unaware of the underlying strategies God is utilizing to direct a person's life. At some point we have to have confidence that, "He who began a good work in you will carry it on to completion…" (Phil. 1:6). We often get reports of people, who at the time, seemed to have had little impact from a Treasure Hunt encounter, only to find out later that the seed that was sown actually took root and began to sprout up later.

GOD'S GOING TO POP YOUR BIG TOE

Recently, one of our Bethel School of Supernatural Ministry teams was out Treasure Hunting and was led to a large retail store where their clues led them to the security guard who worked in the store. After the team had built rapport and explained that God wanted to bless him in some way, the man offered that he was in constant pain because his big toe had been broken for quite some time.

The team prayed for the man at his post in the store for about a minute, but did not get any breakthrough. Not giving up, the team leader explained to the man that she had heard the Lord say that He was going to cause the toe to pop, and that it would be healed. The team went on to encourage the man with some prophetic words, and then left to find some more clues on their Treasure Map.

A few weeks later, the team leader was hosting her daughter's bridal shower. As the young women were talking over cake and punch, one of the bridesmaids began to share with the group that some people had approached her fiancé and had said that his big toe would pop and be healed.

She related that a week later, as he was watching television, his big toe popped and was completely healed. At that very moment, he had full movement of his toe and all of the pain was gone. She went on to say that he had not been a Christian and was not interested in going to church, but since the time of his healing he had been constantly talking about going to his future in-laws' church, where they had been fervently praying for him.

We never know how God is weaving the circumstances of someone's life together for good. At some point, we have to believe that God's Spirit is able to lead people to the right place where they can find the nurture they need to thrive in the Kingdom. It is important to keep in mind that "**the Lord** added to their number daily those who were being saved." It is His desire to direct His newly adopted sons and daughters into the family.

"I'm a Realist"

There are times when we have supernatural encounters with people who are not quite ready to make a full commitment to Christ, let alone the Church. In Acts chapter 26, the apostle Paul was defending himself before Festus, the governor over Judea. At one point, he turned to King Agrippa for support as he asked, "...do you believe the prophets? I know you do" (Acts 26:27).

Agrippa's response is typical of many who have been approached by Treasure Hunters who are attempting to get them into Christ and the Church. He says, "Do you think that in such a short time you can persuade me to be a

Christian?" (Acts 26:28). So many times we forget to realize that some people take longer to process what they have encountered.

Some are like Thomas who, when he put his hands in the holes in Jesus' side and hands, immediately responded, "My Lord and my God" (John 20:28). Others, however, are like Agrippa, who needed further evidence and/or time to believe.

Recently, one of our Bethel School of Supernatural Ministry Treasure Hunt teams were directed to Home Depot, and then aisle 16, where they found a 77-year-old man with a "hip problem," "green jacket," and a "striped shirt."

As it turned out, the man had received a hip replacement eight years prior, but it had not been fitted properly, causing continual pain. The Treasure Hunters asked the man if they could pray for him to be healed, but his response was that he was a "realist" and did not believe in God, let alone that God could heal him. The students responded that they, too, were "realists," and that God "really" could heal him.

At that creative response, the man agreed to let the students pray for him. After a short prayer, one of the students asked how he felt. As he began to move around to test it out, he was surprised to find that he absolutely had no pain in his hip, and he no longer needed the cane he had previously used to help him along.

The same student noticed that the man had hearing aids on both ears and asked if he would like the team to pray for his ears as well. Without hesitation or instruction, the man pulled the hearing aids out and began to converse loudly with the students about the nature of his hearing problem and his desire to be healed.

The team member placed his hands on the man's ears and prayed a short, simple prayer. The man was not immediately healed, so one of the young women on the team began to pray for the man's ears. After a short time, the man began to hear everything the student was praying and asked her to stop yelling. The student explained that she was not yelling, and then both realized that he had been totally healed.

They attempted to lead the man to Christ, but he was so confused at what had happened that he said that he just needed to go home and process. After all, he was a realist. The team gave him a card that had the directions to our church and invited the man to an upcoming evangelistic crusade that we were having at our church the next evening.

The next evening, the man was at the front door of the church waiting for one of the Treasure Hunting team members to show up. One of the students who had prayed for him the previous day found him and invited the man to sit with him. The man confessed that he had gone home and told his wife that he had been healed by God, and his wife had responded that it was not true, but just a hoax. Immediately, the man's hearing was lost again, which is why he showed up at the meeting wearing hearing aides.

During the meeting, there was an invitation for anyone to stand who needed healing. Without hesitation, the man stood to his feet, and his ears were reopened! A short while later, an invitation was given for those who wanted to receive Christ, and the man stood to his feet once again to say "yes" to God's call on his life.

Sometimes, it takes several encounters to connect people into the Church. This Treasure Hunt team could have tried to apply more pressure to get the man to repeat a prayer, but they trusted that God was after Him and would further reveal Himself to him. Like the old adage, "You can run, but you can't hide," so it is with God, and that is a good thing!

God has a way of setting up circumstances and experiences that grab our attention. In fact, the Scriptures are clear, "No one can come to Me unless the Father who sent Me draws him…" (John 6:44). Similarly, in John 6:65, Jesus says, "No one can come to Me unless the Father has enabled him." At some point, we have to trust that the Father is able to do His job. Our only concern should be to release His presence through our lives in practical ways, and invite those we meet to the "banquet."

GOD HAS A WAY OF FINDING THOSE WHO ARE READY

Sometimes, we have the opportunity of encountering people, through even the strangest supernatural encounters, who are absolutely eager to jump into the Treasure Chest. It is an amazing privilege to find someone like this, at just the perfect time, when they are ready to commit themselves to Christ and follow Him through discipleship.

Recently, one of our Treasure Hunt teams went out looking for clues, but after about an hour without finding one clue, one of the students from our School of Supernatural Ministry noticed that all of the clues seemed to point to his unsaved brother who lived in another state. They decided to call him and found that he fit the description of all of the clues on their Treasure Map.

The students began to prophesy to the young man on the other end of the phone, calling out his destiny and the promises of salvation through receiving Christ. The young man was so touched by the prophetic words that revealed the secrets of his heart, that the next day he drove to the church where he met his brother and the Treasure Hunt team.

He gave his heart to the Lord, and all weekend long he encountered the Lord's presence in supernatural encounters as people prophesied and prayed with him. At the end of the weekend, he announced that he was finished with a life of drug addiction and depression. He is now in a discipleship school, while he awaits his enrollment in the School of Supernatural Ministry here at Bethel next fall.

This testimony is an example of how God gets people into the Treasure Chest. In displaying His goodness and kindness toward people, He creates a passion to follow and to do whatever it takes to find Him. In this case, the young man was so transformed by the encounter that he now wants to get trained to be a Treasure Hunter, which is Jesus' ultimate desire of those who find their way into the Treasure Chest.

Once we are born again, we become the light of the world. Jesus taught that it was only natural for a light to shine forth, especially when it is set on top of a hill. The only way for it not to shine is for us to intentionally hide it (Matt. 5:14-16). Amazingly, when we allow the light to shine through our lives, it has an uncanny way of identifying hidden Treasures and drawing those Treasures out of darkness and into the light.

Being a Treasure Hunter is about finding Treasure. Sometimes, our job is to uncover the hidden Treasures, knowing that someone else will come along to pick them up and get them into the Treasure Chest, the Church. But whatever the case, our responsibility is to be witnesses to the ends of the earth, with the goal of making disciples of all nations, which includes every sub-culture and every person. God wants to fill His Treasure Chest up with lost coins. That is our task while here on earth.

Therefore, in order to accomplish this mission, it is imperative that every believer takes personal responsibility to pursue the lost coins that God has purposed for him or her to find. And when they are found and safely stored in the Treasure Chest, the angels in Heaven rejoice, and our Heavenly Father celebrates.

There are still plenty of Treasures to be found. They are in our neighborhoods, our schools, at the dentist office, the post office, at work, the grocery store, and even in our own families. They are everywhere. They are waiting for an Ananias to come and find them so that they can fulfill their God-given destiny. Will you go?

Happy Treasure Hunting!

The Treasure Map

1. **Each person writes down Words of Knowledge in the spaces allowed for each category.**

   • **Location** (stop sign, bench, digital clock, coffee shop, Target, Wal-Mart, etc.).

   _____ _____ _____ _____ _____ _____

   • **A person's name.**

   _____ _____ _____ _____ _____ _____

   • **A person's appearance** (the color of their specific articles of clothing, the color of their hair, etc.).

   _____ _____ _____ _____ _____ _____

   • **What they might need prayer for** (knee brace, cane, kidneys, tumor, left ankle, marriage, etc.).

   _____ _____ _____ _____ _____

   • **The unusual** (lollipop, windmill, lime-green door, dolphins, etc.).

   _____ _____ _____ _____ _____

2. Form groups of three or four.

- Combine the *words of knowledge* of the group to make your "Treasure Map."

***Note: Each member keeps their own list—*do not* combine lists on a separate sheet.

3. Choose a beginning location (compare other clues on the way to your first location).

4. Start looking for the treasure.

5. When you find something on the Treasure Map (taken from the individual maps in the group)...

Approach the person.

- Say something like: "This may seem a little odd, but we're on a treasure hunt and we think you're on our list."
- Show them your list. (It may be one or two things from each list, or just one thing from one list.)
- Build rapport. (Make friends—ask questions about them to get to know them.)
- Let them know that God has highlighted them, and wants to bless them.
- Pay attention for things that you can help them with, and ask if you can pray for them.

6. If they say "No"...

- Build more rapport (common ground—friendship).
- Ask the Holy Spirit what He wants to highlight about the person.
- Give them some encouraging words (*prophesy*) without being religious.

7. Ask again if you can pray for them.

- If they say "No"—Bless them and proceed to the next Treasure (*person*).
- If they say "Yes" (especially for healing)...
  — Ask for the presence of God to come. (*Release His presence on them.*)
  — Command the pain to leave, bones to be set, back to be realigned, tumor to shrink, etc.
  — Ask them to test it out: "Do something that you couldn't do before we prayed."
  — Repeat if necessary.

8. When they are healed, or you have blessed them through prophetic words...

- Explain what just happened (*the kindness of God revealed—He knows you and cares about you, etc.*).
- Ask them if they would like to know Jesus personally (*have a relationship with Him*).
- Help them to ask Jesus into their life.

9. Go to the next Divine Appointment on the Treasure Map!

THE USE OF THE TREASURE MAP

1. Fold the map in half from top to bottom so that only your clues are facing you.

2. Fold the map again from side to side so that half of your clues are on one side of the fold while the other half is on the other side. This makes the map less conspicuous, while still giving the Treasure Hunter visibility to all of the clues on the map by simply pivoting it by rotating the hand. This may sound a little silly or overboard, but I have found that being as discreet as possible is more effective than drawing a lot of attention to the Treasure Hunting group, especially in a store or business.

3. Make sure each Treasure Hunter keeps their map available and accessible to each person on the team. Many clues are found by looking on another team member's map.

4. Do not put the map in your pocket, backpack, or purse. You know the saying, "Out of sight, out of mind." Most people who do not find Treasure are the ones who do not use their map consistently.

5. The Treasure Map is like a puzzle, requiring concentration and creativity to put together.

6. You can approach someone who only has one clue on your Map. Often, you will find that they possess other clues once you begin to build rapport and ask penetrating questions.

7. Utilize creativity and imagination. For example, "post office" could be a mailbox, a mail delivery person, a mail store, the post office, or even a letter that someone is

about to mail. A person's name could mean a friend, relative, an acquaintance who needs prayer, reconciliation, or some other point of significance, or certainly could be the name of the person you have approached.

8. Once you find the clues, make sure you show them the map. Remember, for most people, "Seeing is believing."

9. Approach people in twos or threes at the most. A large group can be intimidating. It is also less threatening for the person you are approaching if the genders are mixed. I usually do not like to take more than five people on a Treasure Hunt because normally five can fit into one vehicle easily. Out of the group, I will also choose two of one gender and three of the other.

10. Children are great to have on Treasure Hunts. They are less threatening, and often have much better "out of the box" creativity to find clues.

11. Do not split your group of five up for more than one encounter. Work as a team and continually touch base, checking your clues and changing the team members who are approaching potential Treasures.

12. The instructions for conducting a divine encounter are on the opposite side of the initial fold you made with your map. Have each person on the team read these instructions before launching out.

13. Once you have a divine encounter with someone, write the testimony on the back of the Map. Keep them for later encouragement of what God has done through you, and what He will do.

A Healing Ministry Model

Getting Started

1. Ask the person to briefly tell you: what's wrong or what do they want?

2. If appropriate, ask them if you can place your hand on the area that needs healing (optional).

3. Ask for God's presence *(His Kingdom to come).*

4. Listen for the Holy Spirit's promptings to pray in certain ways and various strategies (take risk).

5. Look for visible signs/manifestations (noticing what God is doing *in* and *on* them).

6. Ask them if they are feeling any sensations going on in their body (heat, cold, peace, electricity, etc.).

7. Ask them to check it out/to do something they couldn't do before (try to cause the pain they experienced before).

8. If healed, rejoice with them and give praise to God.

9. Encourage them to get a doctor's report.

IF NO BREAKTHROUGH IN HEALING...

1. Thank God for anything that is going on. *(Thankfulness often releases greater breakthrough.)*

2. Pray for increase and thank Him for the increase of His presence and healing.

3. Declare healing promises over them (Scriptures, testimonies).

4. Repeat steps 7 through 9.

IF PAIN GETS WORSE OR MOVES AS YOU'RE PRAYING...

1. Possible spirit of affliction/infirmity.

2. Take authority over the spirit (you do not need to yell, let them vomit, etc.).

3. Release more healing presence.

IF NO BREAKTHROUGH OR PAIN INCREASES...

1. Ask them if there may be someone they need to forgive.

2. If yes, ask them to forgive them out loud.

3. If no, pray again, and release more of God's presence on them.

4. Begin to prophesy hope and destiny over them (some people do not feel worthy to be healed).

5. Ask them to check it out again (do something they could not do before—something that caused pain).

IF STILL NO BREAKTHROUGH...

1. Always encourage them that God is good and is in a good mood.

2. Always encourage them to continue to pursue breakthrough (when we pray, His Kingdom comes, and when His Kingdom comes, good things happen, because He is a good God in a good mood).

3. Encourage them to give thanks for what they do see or feel, even if they have only experienced a small measure of breakthrough.

4. Always bless them.

5. *Never* lay the responsibility on them, even if they are resistant to healing and have no or little faith.

6. Let the Holy Spirit do His work.